The Joy

of

Lent

Compiled and Edited by
Pat McDonough

Resurrection Press
An Imprint of
CATHOLIC BOOK PUBLISHING CO.
Totowa • New Jersey

DEDICATION

For Mom
1919 - 2002

— · — · — · —

Scripture quotations are from THE JERUSALEM BIBLE, copyright © 1966 by Darton, Longman & Todd, Ltd. and Doubleday, a division of Bantam, Doubleday, Dell Publishing Group, Inc. Reprinted by permission.

First published in March, 2003 by Resurrection Press, Catholic Book Publishing Company.

ISBN 1-878718-77-0

Library of Congress Catalog Number: 2002115854

Cover design by Beth DeNapoli

Printed in Canada.

1 2 3 4 5 6 7 8 9

Acknowledgements

I would like to extend my gratitude to all the authors who took the time to reflect on the season of Lent and its meaning in their lives. Special thanks to my husband, Tony, without whose help I could not have completed this project. And my deepest gratitude to Emilie, whose patience and encouragement surpassed anything I could have expected.

Contents

Acknowledgements   3

Introduction   6

Ash Wednesday   9

First Sunday of Lent   14

Second Sunday of Lent   24

Third Sunday of Lent   35

Fourth Sunday of Lent   50

Fifth Sunday of Lent   65

Passion Sunday   79

Easter   92

Introduction

I LIKE LENT, not only because it signals that spring is on the way. I like Lent for a lot of reasons.

I like ashes. They remind me of who I am and to whom I belong. I am Christ's. I belong to a church that belongs to Him. I'm one of millions who walked into a church last Wednesday, tired of winter and spiritually half asleep. I left the church with a cross of ashes on my head. The words, "Turn away from sin and be faithful to the Gospel" were on my mind. My ashes and everyone else's, remind me that I need a support group to help me stay with the program. I have one. It has a billion members. It's called the Catholic church.

Remember those little mite boxes we used to get? Anytime I came across a few coins, I put them in the box for the children who had no food, no clothes, no toys. In the days of mite boxes, I gave as much as 90 percent of my income (allowance and other coins that came my way) to the poor. I haven't given that much of my income to charity since. Tithing can be tough today, but back then, I guess I was more generous. I liked those mite boxes. They brought out the best in me.

I like the color purple. Hermann Rorschach wrote a lot about colors and the important role that they play in surfacing emotion. Purple evokes sadness and a solemn tone. It keeps me focused on the journey toward Calvary. It helps to have it on the altar.

I like Lenten gospels. The characters are so real and so memorable. When I was about five, I had an illustrated book of the Bible. The Temptation of Jesus, which is always read on the first Sunday of Lent, was vividly illustrated. Satan had a long red tail, pointed teeth and horns. I was terrified. I still am. It's not so much the hideous creature with the tail that scares me today, but demons in general, especially mine.

I like Lent because I have to make a conscious effort *not* to greet the gospel with an alleluia. I'm aware that something is missing and I feel as if I have to start looking for what's lost. That's a good way to feel in Lent.

I like Lent because it gives me the opportunity to say to my kids, "It's Lent. Let's think about what we can do differently." They reluctantly give it some thought and this year they've come up with some pretty good ideas. I like when the church helps me guide my kids toward something greater than CDs. Lent helps me shift their attention from computers and clothes to something a little more substantial.

I like Lent because St. Patrick's Day falls in the middle of it and I always feel the need for a break by March 17th. And I like St. Joseph's table because it provides a respite from fasting.

I don't like fasting, especially in the winter when carbohydrates call out to me from every corner of the house. Fasting forces me to examine my most basic activities. That's when my body and soul start to wrestle with each other's urges. My unholy diet is called into question; the ice cream and hot fudge, the cookies and brownies. Thinking about the things my body craves forces me to think about my spiritual cravings, too. Maybe my desire for chocolate is biologically based, but maybe it's a substitute for deeper longings. In an attempt to marry mind and mouth, heart, soul and body, I'll forgo the chocolate; the

Ring Dings and Oreos, the Godiva and the brownies, too. Oh, the brownies. . . .

I like Palm Sunday. I love the reading of the Passion, the dramatic way that the whole church enters into this story. I look forward to the Triduum and its beautiful rituals. The stripping of the altar on Holy Thursday always leaves me feeling as empty as the tabernacle. I'm reminded to strip away all the leftover, last minute things that keep me from God.

I like Good Friday. It's unlike any other day of the year. I like the veneration of the cross. I like the Stations of the Cross, too. I feel more in step with Jesus when I walk the steps that he walked to Calvary.

I like Lent. It's like an old friend with whom I can argue year after year and know that I'm a better person for being challenged. I like what Lent does to me. Its grace forms me and transforms me time and time again.

My love for Lent inspired this book. I wanted to know what other people thought about during these forty days. Do they fast? Do they pray? Do they honor Lent in a way I haven't thought about? I asked forty people in my life to share their thoughts on the Lenten readings. I hope you enjoy reading their responses as much as I did.

ASH WEDNESDAY

"Come back to me with your heart, fasting, weeping, mourning"   *Joel 2:12*

HOW CAN WE EVER FORGET the Twin Tower collapse, people fleeing for their lives, ashes clinging to faces, hair, clothing and even lungs. *"Remember that you are ashes and unto ashes you shall return."* Ash Wednesday invites us to an anointing with a smudge of ash that is no sign of pride and privilege but a renewed call to courageous compassion.

Beyond the ashen fog of Ground Zero, life has many other ways of confronting us with our vulnerability, our utter helplessness. The fearsomeness of such weakness, whether known in public confrontation or felt as quiet shackle, screams for encouragement. Anointing involves courage and strength. Ash Wednesday does not initiate some prideful gesture, nor negativistic beating up on self, but an ashen anointing for courage in the midst of our shared vulnerability. Purple, Lent's color, when properly appreciated, radiates courage and strength rather than sad disappointment.

The anointing with a smudge of ash trumpets the central conversion of Lent. More than a conversion away from sin, though this is surely involved, a call to greater compassion inaugurates the forty days. This time of special compassion always spotlights God, whose loving compassion is faithfully fleshed in Jesus.

But how do we stir up in ourselves this compassion of Lent? We learn quickly that we cannot strong arm our way to compassion. As long as we fail to embrace our basic fragility and helplessness, mature compassion eludes us. Beyond our helplessness, there is need for surprising Good News: the Good News of God's Love revealed in the very depths of our vulnerability. This brings encouragement beyond our own power and makes possible compassion—that enticing ability to reach out and suffer with another. Compassion, therefore, is born in our discovery of love often hidden in the shrouds of our weakness. In this way we must be loved into compassion through the love both of God and of our brothers and sisters.

"Repent and believe the Good News" is the haunting invitation of Lent. It takes expression in an anointing for courage and compassion in the midst of our common vulnerability. So Lent always has more to teach us: not fearfully to flee our helplessness but to find a love that moves us out to the other suffering people. In this way, Lent is always a special season anointing us, not for pride and privilege, but for courage in compassion that renews the Body of Christ now in our midst.

George Aschenbrenner is co-founder of the Institute for Priestly Formation and the author of several books including Quickening the Fire in Our Midst: The Challenge of Diocesan Priestly Spirituality *(Loyola Press, 2002).*

THURSDAY AFTER ASH WEDNESDAY

"Choose life, then, so that you and your descendants may live in the love of Yahweh your God, obeying his voice, holding fast to him." Deuteronomy 30:19-20

I AM THE MOTHER OF SIX children, and with each child, I certainly felt as if I was choosing life. But bringing a baby into the world is only one way of choosing life. I have tried to teach all my children to love the Lord, to heed his commandments, and to hold fast to him in good times and bad. I've encouraged my kids to choose their friends with care, choose thoughtfully how they spend their time, what movies they see and what books they read.

Lent presents us with a reason to re-think our choices. Are we really choosing life in our home, in our leisure, in the way we spend our money? Do we take the time to listen to each other and to love each other or does more of our time go into things like the computer and TV? Occasionally, it does, at least in my house. That's why Lent is so important. It challenges us to change, to abandon our lazy habits and transform our lives. Last year, we participated in a March for Life. As a family, we found an activity that demonstrates one way in which we choose life. We also found a lot of time to talk to one another while we marched. When we choose life, God chooses to bless our lives abundantly.

Marianne McDonald is a nurse and homemaker living in West Virginia.

FRIDAY AFTER ASH WEDNESDAY

"They seek me day after day, they long to know my ways."   *Isaiah 58:2*

LENT, FOR ME, is not only a time of spiritual discipline, prayer and renewal in preparation for Easter. It has also presented an opportunity for intellectual exploration and an even greater understanding of the role that Christianity has played in my personal life.

During Lent I participated in my parish sponsored Wednesday evening suppers followed by classes with members of the community as well as religious scholars. Beyond Bible reading and discussion, people were called on to interpret the sacrifice of Jesus in their own lives. Could we all be more giving? Or, are we content with the good life professing to be a Christian with no real time to deal with those less fortunate? The discussions always caused us to think, and hopefully, to carry the teachings of Christ into a real world so desperately in need of more justice, kindness, charity and forgiveness.

In addition to the spiritual and intellectual aspects of those Wednesday evening sessions, each of us developed a better sense of bonding with one another as friends in Christ. The Lenten period came alive in a manner that I had not experienced before participating in these lively exchanges.

Robert McMillan co-hosts "Face Off" on WLIW and is an attorney in private practice on Long Island.

SATURDAY AFTER ASH WEDNESDAY

"I have come to call not the upright but sinners to repentance."

Luke 5:32

LENT IS FOR PEOPLE LIKE ME. I'm probably a good person, but not without my faults. Ask my husband and kids. They'll be able to rattle off my shortcomings in sixty seconds flat. OK, I admit it. I'm a sinner. That's why I love Lent. It was made for people like me.

"O God, you are yourself eternal joy. From us you never depart, yet we, with difficulty, return to you." St. Augustine penned these words in *Confessions*, his personal reflection on sin and conversion.

God is eternal joy. He is Easter. He is the Resurrection, and while I believe this, my actions sometimes contradict my theology. Like Augustine, I've often departed from the ways of the Lord, but somehow, with great difficulty and great grace, I find my way back. The journey back is Lent. It's turning around, changing direction and heading back home to the God who loves me more than I love myself.

Jackie DeGenero graduated from Penn State with a degree in physical education. Today she is a poet, the mother of three teenagers and working towards a degree in theology.

FIRST SUNDAY OF LENT

Year A   *Matthew 4:1-11*
Year B   *Mark 1:12–15*
Year C   *Luke 4:1-13*

I WAS PROBABLY no more than three years old the first time I heard the story of Creation. I was captivated by the colorful cast of characters who roamed the Garden of Eden, a magical and mystical place where God played with clay and formed creatures who looked like me, a place where serpents spoke, and in doing so, changed the course of history. This was a wonderful story, told and retold to my delight. But unlike the other stories my mother told me back then, this one didn't have a happy ending. Why? "Because Adam and Eve gave into temptation," my mother said.

My mother, who by her own description, was a staunch, Irish Catholic, told me that temptation should be met with nothing less than self-control. My mother coined the phrase, *"Just Say No"* long before Nancy Reagan launched her campaign against drugs. My first impulse upon hearing the Lenten gospel of the temptation of Jesus is to recall my mother's words of warning. But the more I think about it, the more I wonder if these stories are really not about self-control, but rather, self-surrender.

It has long been the custom of Catholics to practice self-control throughout Lent by sacrificing something that we enjoy, an everyday temptation without which our lives would somehow be diminished. I thought about giving up Godiva, without which my life would be substantially less pleasurable. But the truth is, I tumble into temptations far more treacherous than the fruits of the cacao bush every day. My religious impulse to give up Belgium's best may be a poor attempt to camouflage the things I really need to give up, like gossip and grudges, and growling at my kids. Giving up chocolate could be a substitute for giving of myself, for giving up my pride, my stubbornness, and far reaching foolishness, all of which can be far more devastating than a chocolate covered cherry.

Giving up Godiva brings me to a hiding place rather than a holy place. We can hide behind religious rituals and practices that don't really challenge us and certainly don't change us. Lent doesn't live in those hiding places; it dies there. Lent lives in self-surrender, the places of kindness and courage, compassion and mercy; the places where we are stretched, and ultimately changed. That's not to say that fasting, prayer and almsgiving are without purpose, but in my mind, they need to be re-imagined in light of who I am today and what I need to make this Lenten journey one worth taking.

Thomas Merton said the only journey worth taking is the journey inward. Lent finds life in self-discovery and in the acceptance of who we are; creatures fashioned in the image of our Creator, people who are like God, but not God. Adam and Eve missed the point. The most dangerous demon in the garden wasn't a slippery serpent, but themselves, a man and woman who wanted to be God more than they wanted to be human. They lacked self-knowledge and the ability to accept the wonderful gift of humanity, limitations and all. Because they had their eyes on something other than their relationship with God, they were easily lured by the serpent's words.

Jesus understood who he was. He was a human being who surrendered himself in relationship to God and others. He surrendered power and glory for the experience of love, a love that brought healing, forgiveness, and salvation to the world.

Perhaps the penitential season of Lent provides us with an opportunity to enter into a process of self-evaluation. These forty days can be a time when we can begin to search for the serpents and demons in our lives. Chances are we don't have to look too far. They're not out there, they're within.

MONDAY OF THE FIRST WEEK OF LENT
"Love your neighbor as yourself."   *Leviticus 19:18*

WHATEVER ITS ANCIENT ORIGINS, the Lenten season of my youth was a time for prayer and penance, mostly in the form of denial. Because its purpose wasn't always sharply defined, the emphasis of denial naturally projected an attitude of expressed guilt and the need for learning forgiveness. It was assumed to be a time to sublimate our human appetites, probably as a reminder that they were invariably temptations to be excessive.

Giving up things you didn't really like anyway, was a childish way of fooling oneself into thinking our Lenten obligation had been met.

My sense is that together with many of the practices of the '40s and '50s, like Benediction, the Stations of the Cross and the Rosary, commitment to Lenten practices has withered. This might be a good time to renew observance with a New Millennium emphasis on the positive instead of the negative. Why not commit to forty days of reminding ourselves of the Glory of Easter about to come—the

Resurrection? Why not commit ourselves to a fresh look at the essence of Christianity, which is loving one another as we love ourselves for the love of ultimate truth? How about a good deed a day, an act of charity, a kind thought, forgiveness of a slight, apologizing for an unkindness, righting a wrong. Think up forty ways to say "I love you Lord." One a day for forty days; then have a good meal with the family on Easter Sunday.

Mario Cuomo served as the Governor of New York State from 1982–1994.

TUESDAY OF THE FIRST WEEK OF LENT
"Your will be done"   *Matthew 6:10*

LENT CALLS TO MIND will power and, in this corner, the lack of it. When I was a boy in the '40s and '50s, Catholic kids were urged to give up something from Ash Wednesday to Easter, to make a sacrifice for the Lord. I tried to quit candy, but failed. Sweets were irresistible to weak-willed little Billy. As a young man in the '60s, I vowed to abstain from alcohol for Lent, a truly heroic sacrifice. Ash Wednesday passed without temptation, and Thursday, likewise, but Friday was pizza night and pizza without beer was impossible for a fellow whose Lenten commitment didn't match his craving for gratification. My resolve to forego alcohol for forty days lasted just two.

"You have no will power," a friend said. I fiercely resented him for saying that. Red in the face, I denied it was so. More than forty years later I still can feel how it hurt to hear the truth about myself.

I was humiliated but not humbled. Humiliation helps some of us along the way but it doesn't get us there overnight. Time and again we're brought low by pride, greed, lust, anger, gluttony, envy, sloth. Addiction to alcohol or drugs or gambling or food or sex or possessions defeat us. Fear makes us miserable. Resentment ruins our day. We love ourselves too much and others not enough. We identify with how Peter must have felt after denying Jesus three times—like a failure.

Failure is a hard way to a deeper faith, but spiritual progress for some of us always begins with powerlessness. "When I am weak, then I am strong," St. Paul said. We wish we were self-disciplined souls with sturdy spiritual lives built on decades of successful Lents, but the truth is that asceticism eludes us. Oh, I quit candy eventually, but will power had nothing to do with it. I developed an allergy to chocolate that caused excruciating headaches. And alcohol went out of my life, too, but only after years of abusing it and not because I resolutely said no. The stuff finally made me so sick in body and soul that sobering up felt better than drinking. That was the divine plan for saving a guy with no will power.

Some of us are glad to believe in a merciful God and not in ourselves. "Thy will be done, God, not mine." A resolution I make at Lent is to try to spend more time in church, at Mass and services such as the Stations of the Cross. I try to go in a spirit of gratitude for God's blessings and humility for doing nothing to deserve them. After all these years I still lack will power, but I believe that God's will is powerful enough for both of us.

Bill Reel's column on religious issues is syndicated in newspapers throughout the United States.

WEDNESDAY OF THE FIRST WEEK OF LENT

"Sacrifices give you no pleasure, burnt offering you do not desire. Sacrifice to God is a broken spirit, a broken, contrite heart."   *Psalm 51:16-17*

WHEN I BEGAN MY MINISTRY to the students of Brown University and The Rhode Island School of Design in 1999, I invited them to create The Stations of the Cross for our worship space. A sophomore named Nicole painted the scene of Peter denying Jesus.

A few months later she wrote about her experience:

> Depicting one of the Stations of the Cross forced to me to approach painting in a new way. This painting was not just for me; it was for others and, in a sense, for God. I felt I couldn't paint in the way I normally did, which was to just start and see what happened. I had to plan. I ended up thinking myself into circles. As Good Friday loomed near, there was still no painting nor was I closer to feeling ready to start. With a prayer for guidance—and prevention against terrible blunders—I just started painting. When I stopped trying to plan and control, everything dovetailed together beautifully. I was reminded that I had been trying too hard to control and plan everything of late. I had forgotten what I once knew, that prayer does do something, and that if you let him, God sees to it that things work out for the best, even if you don't always know it at the

time. Painting one of the Stations of the
Cross has helped me to grow as an artist, as
a Catholic, and as a person.

The Lenten practice of prayer, along with fasting and
almsgiving, is a vital part of how this season can move us
to once again return to God. To return fully to God—
bringing along our wounded, sinful, controlling, hardened selves—we need a long period of time, a lifetime
really, but seven weeks of Lent is a good start. As Nicole
reminds us, it is the act of surrender that makes possible a
genuine transformation of heart.

*Mary Beth Reynolds is the Catholic Campus Minister at Brown
University and Rhode Island School of Design.*

THURSDAY OF THE FIRST WEEK OF LENT
"I thank you, Yahweh, with all my heart."

Psalm 138:1

MOST PEOPLE THINK that Lent is all about giving up things,
making sacrifices that make us miserable, as if God wants
to see us suffer for His sake. On the contrary, I think God
wants less suffering and more sharing, greater joy and
abundant love of our neighbors. I imagine God in heaven
wishing the world could return to the first days of
Creation. Maybe Lent is a time to return to God and His
plan for the world.

About three years ago I decided to use the forty days
to find forty ways to remain faithful to the world that God
created. I started with small things like getting up before
my wife and cooking breakfast for the family. That brings

us all together for breakfast rather than everyone grabbing something while they're running out the door. We all leave a little more fortified for the day in front of us. Maybe we have more to bring to school and work that day, feeling a little more nourished. Maybe we can lighten someone's load later in the day.

I've got the kids recycling around the house, teaching them the importance of remaining faithful to God's plan for Creation. We participated in their school's effort to clean up the beach, removing cans and bottles from the shore in an effort to protect marine life. We also sponsored a spring clean up of the parish grounds last year in the hope of heightening everyone's awareness of protecting our planet.

On a personal level, I go to Mass every Lenten morning. There, I share myself with others who all share in the Paschal Mystery. On my way to work, I stop to pick up fresh fruit for my co-workers. People gather to grab some grapes or a banana between phone calls and customers. We share a few minutes that otherwise would not have been shared. Maybe this is what God had in mind—people talking and laughing and building community. I try to play my part.

My favorite Lenten ritual is lighting the purple candle that sits on our dinner table throughout Lent. My wife plans simple meals using only non-processed foods. We join hands and give thanks for all of Creation, grateful to be a part of it.

Joe Ruggerio is a teacher living in Long Beach, California.

FRIDAY OF THE FIRST WEEK OF LENT

"If you are bringing your offering to the altar and there remember that your brother has something against you, leave your offering there before the altar, go and be reconciled with your brother first, and then come back and present your offering."

Matthew 5:23-24

IN GOLF, IT'S A MULLIGAN. In child's games, it's a do-over. In life, it's a fresh start. What a great gift to be able to begin again; the smoothing of a relationship that has gone bumpy or the opportunities of a new job. To accept Lent as the time for a new beginning does not have to mean that everyone has some deep, choking sin to turn from. For some, this may be the case.

For many, Lent is the time to grow in trust that humankind was reconciled to God through Jesus Christ; to realize more deeply that our community, whether family or parish or church, is always on the move and called to recommitment and the acceptance of responsibility; to accept more intimately how deeply personal is God's love and forgiveness and to acknowledge that acceptance of this is sincere only when it spills over into our love and forgiveness toward others.

Bishop Emil Wcela serves as an auxiliary in the Diocese of Rockville Centre on Long Island. He is also the author of several books on scripture and a regular columnist in The Long Island Catholic *newspaper.*

SATURDAY OF THE FIRST WEEK OF LENT

"I say this to you, love your enemies and pray for those who persecute you." Matthew 5:44

I'VE ALWAYS HAD TROUBLE with the idea of loving my enemies and praying for those who have hurt me. When I was growing up, my mother would remind me to make an effort to overlook injuries and get on with life.

Today, in an age of terrorism, the temptation to retaliate against terrorist organizations is overwhelming. But do we then become the enemy? Will we be the ones that mothers and children around the world come to fear?

Because the weapons of the 21st century are so lethal, we need to heed the words of the gospel more attentively than ever before. Love our enemies? I found that difficult at age ten. At age fifty, I find it even harder. Love those who have brought such suffering and death to our families and friends and neighbors? I'm not sure I have it in me. But this is our gospel. This is the faith I claim to embrace.

Love my enemies? If not now, when?

Dan Halloran is a mechanic living and working in Madison, Wisconsin.

SECOND SUNDAY OF LENT

Year A   **Matthew 17:1-9**
Year B   **Mark 9:2–10**
Year C   **Luke 9:28–36**

MY FATHER DIED just minutes before I arrived at the hospital with my husband. I stood at my father's deathbed and gazed upon his face. I held his hand and kissed his forehead. And then something remarkable happened. The words of the Lenten gospel began pounding in my head, *"This is my beloved son."*

This was not my beloved son. This was my father. Why were the words, "beloved son" coming to mind?

My father looked different in death than he had in life. The man who once stood six feet tall, and at times appeared even larger than life, no longer looked like Dad. He had been transfigured in death. He had forsaken the many roles he had held in this life, and surrendered, finally and completely, to the will of God. Complete surrender changed him.

I regret that I was not with him in his final moments and that I will never know his final thoughts, but I know this: I was extraordinarily blessed to have had the opportunity to see him in this light, perhaps in the same light in which God saw him throughout his entire life. Is it possible that we are never anything more in God's eyes than sons and daughters who are beloved, regardless of our achievements, our possessions, our positions in life?

I imagine that my experience was not unlike that of the apostles who accompanied Jesus to the mountaintop. There they were given the opportunity to see Jesus in a new light, perhaps the same light in which God saw him. The man whom they admired, the man who cured the sick and raised the dead, who walked on water and brought sight to the blind, was seen by God, first and foremost, not as a prophet, not as a teacher, but simply as a beloved son. Jesus was transfigured and the apostles were transformed. Their experience on the mountaintop was, like my own, one of revelation; a new vision, a graced encounter.

Is their experience any different from our experiences of falling in love, when both the lover and the beloved are transfigured in each other's eyes and transformed by the experience? We are, time and time again, transformed by the miracle of love, of marriage, of parenthood, intimacy and friendship. These are miracles of no less stature than what occurred on the mountaintop in Israel 2000 years ago. They are experiences of human love that offer the possibility of transformation and conversion because they are, most likely, also experiences of divine love, the same love that God holds for His beloved Son and for us, His beloved children.

We are offered new insight into ourselves, into others, and into the mystery of God through our relationships, particularly our most intimate relationships. It's more than happenstance that the story of the Transfiguration is found among the Lenten readings. Lent is a time when we're asked to take another look at ourselves, our spouses and children, those whom we love and those whom we refuse to love. It's a time to reconsider our lives, our choices, the decisions we've made and those still begging our attention. Lent asks us to look at our lives in a new light with the possibility of a new perspective—God's perspective.

MONDAY OF THE SECOND WEEK OF LENT

"Be compassionate just as your Father is compassionate. Do not judge, and you will not be judged; do not condemn, and you will not be condemned; forgive, and you will be forgiven."

Luke 6:36-37

LUKE INSTRUCTS ME TO FORGIVE, or pardon, but also warns me not to judge; but judging is something I *have* to do. That is the vocation, or role, I've accepted in society. In carrying out that role, frequently, I look to scripture for strength. " . . . give your servant a heart to understand how to govern your people, how to discern between good and evil. . . ." (1 Kings 3:9). The author must have been a poet. Understanding is normally associated with the mind. We understand something when our thought process makes it clear to us. Heart, however, is usually associated with emotion or passion, or in its purest form, with love. Together the words understand and heart, like terrible beauty, speak volumes.

But getting back to our call to forgive, as a judge, forgiveness is not something I can dispense. I can try to foster it in the hearts of crime-victims, but it is not an easy item to sell to someone who has been victimized—whether it be a battered spouse, a young woman who has been raped, or the grieving parent of a teenager who has been murdered for no reason. It seems pretty futile, and in fact, insensitive, for a judge to tell these victims and survivors that they should forgive the convicted defendants who are about to be sentenced. Most times they are too angry to even think of forgiveness.

Part of the problem is that forgiveness is difficult to define. As noted recently by Avery Cardinal Dulles in an article on forgiveness in *America* magazine (Oct 7, 2002) "Christians are generally confused about its meaning and application."

So, in Lent, when I read Luke's direction to forgive, I turn to the wisdom of John Paul II when he states: ". . . there can be no peace without justice, and no justice without forgiveness."

That is what I try to do, i.e., be fair, be just. Try to be sensitive to the frailty of those appearing before me—to the fact that they may lack education, discipline, structure, and, in most cases, support. There but for the grace of God. . . .

Honorable Michael F. Mullen is a graduate of Fairfield University and St. John's Law School, where he was a Thomas More scholar. He was appointed to the bench in 1987 and sits in Supreme Court in Riverhead, New York.

TUESDAY OF THE SECOND WEEK OF LENT

"Anyone who raises himself up will be humbled, and anyone who humbles himself will be raised up."
Matthew 23:12

I ONCE HEARD A BRIEF HOMILY on these words. After the gospel, the priest simply said, "I think the words of today's gospel are the most frightening ones Jesus ever spoke for those of us who are ordained."

That was twenty years ago. Perhaps the priest knew then what we all know now. Some of our church leaders have abused power to such a degree that the whole church has been thrown into crisis. Rather than protecting the lives of those they claim to shepherd, some of our leaders have chosen to protect their own interests, and in doing so, put the lives of many, and certainly, the life of the church, in jeopardy.

This Lenten gospel is a stark reminder that we, the church, and we, the individuals that make up the church, are in need of conversion. Individual conversion, as well as institutional conversion, is called for in these forty days of Lent, perhaps more than ever before. When Jesus says that those who raise themselves up will be humbled, he is talking about the scribes and Pharisees who love to take their places of honor at banquets and to be called by titles of respect, but their words are many and their deeds are few. How many of our religious leaders would pass the gospel's litmus test?

The good news is that many would pass. The bad news is that too many would not. There are many bishops who, like Oscar Romero, live their lives in solidarity with the poor, and who lay down their lives for their people. They can be found in Central and South America, the Philippines and Asia. The developed nations also have bishops who hear the voices of their people and try to shepherd them as humble servants. But every once in a while, I've come across a collar who sees himself, not as a humble servant but more as a medieval prince. If Jesus is correct, those who have raised themselves up will be humbled, maybe by the gospel, maybe by personal faith, in the worse case scenario, by scandal and personal sin.

If these thoughts sound like an anti-institutional jag, they're not meant to be. They're simply a reminder that the leaders of the community are often in situations that carry great temptations. Power brings with it both privilege and responsibility. Today's gospel has a special importance for all of us, especially those of us who publicly proclaim the gospel.

The author is a priest in Boston, Massachusetts.

WEDNESDAY OF THE SECOND WEEK OF LENT
"Into your hands I commit my spirit."   Psalm 31:5

I REMEMBER READING about an ecumenical dialogue between Christians and Buddhists that took place at a Benedictine monastery. Monks from both traditions talked about prayer and spirituality, love, compassion and justice. Many reported that a knowledge of the other tradition enriched their own faith. The Buddhist monks found their Christian counterparts to be soul mates in many ways, but one. They were baffled by the image of Jesus on the cross. It's difficult to see the connection between the image of the crucified Christ and the enlightened Buddha.

Today's psalm is the last prayer uttered by Jesus on the cross. The death of Jesus is so much more than the end of his physical life—it is the culmination of his spiritual life. For Jesus it was in life, and in death, that he could say, "into your hands I commit my spirit." For Christians, the cross means that God has entered into our humanity completely. In the crucified Christ, we see the depths of humanity and the depths of inhumanity. We discover how deeply a human being can love and how darkly human beings can destroy the very love that seeks to save them.

We believe in a God who united Himself to us, not by joining a country club or a corporation, not by being associated with a certain cathedral or prestigious college. We believe in a God who is revealed as suffering, redemptive love and who meets us in hospitals and nursing homes, battlefields and cemeteries. Is Christ the symbol of only the best things in life or has Christ entered our humanity so fully that no dimension of human experience remains outside God's grace and redemption?

On the cross, we find a God in solidarity with all human suffering. On the cross, we find the ultimate expression of a life lived in absolute and total trust in God. On the cross is a life that ended in betrayal and pain. Why is the cross so crucial to our faith. The word *crucial* comes from the Latin word *crux*, or cross. The cross poses a crucial question, not just in Lent, but every day: what do we live for and what are we willing to die for?

Chris McCann is a social worker living in Vermont with his wife and seven children.

THURSDAY OF THE SECOND WEEK OF LENT
"Blessed is anyone who trusts in Yahweh."

Jeremiah 17:7

FOR JEWS, CHRISTIANS AND MUSLIMS alike, Abraham is the exemplar of the believer: trusting in the promise, he follows the voice of God calling him to set out on unknown paths. Faith helps us to discover the signs of God's loving presence in creation, in people, in the events of history and above all in the work and message of Christ, as he inspires people to look beyond themselves, beyond appearances, towards that transcendence where the mystery of God's love for every creature is revealed.

During Lent, everyone—rich and poor—is invited to make Christ's love present through generous works of charity. Our charity is called in a particular way to manifest Christ's love to our brothers and sisters who lack the necessities of life, who suffer hunger, violence or injustice. It is my hope that Christians at every level will become promoters of practical initiatives to ensure an equitable distribution of resources and the promotion of the complete human development of every individual.

"I am with you always . . ." These words of Jesus assure us that in proclaiming and living the gospel of charity we are not alone. Once again, during Lent, he invites us to return to the Father, who is waiting for us with open arms to transform us into living effective signs of his merciful love.

From Lent 2000 *a homily by Pope John Paul II.*

FRIDAY OF THE SECOND WEEK OF LENT
"Remember the marvels He has done." **Psalm 105:5**

RABBI ABRAHAM JOSHUA HESCHEL once said that the whole Bible can be summed up in one word: *remember.* The Jews were a people who remembered their history, their heroes, God's miracles and marvels. Christians are also a people of shared memory. We memorialize Jesus at Mass every day. We remember his mission through the readings, his sacrifice through the Eucharist.

Suppose your house is burning down and you only have enough time to grab one item before running out the door. What do you save? Many people would grab the family photo albums. Those photos are so much more than paper. They're our memories. They're our past. They're our lives. They're who we are.

I have the great good fortune to be married to a woman who knows the importance of memories. She has been running around with the video camera since the kids were in diapers capturing those memories for time eternal. When my fourteen year old daughter is being a fourteen year old daughter, sometimes it helps to remember, to recall and to relive the marvels of her earlier days. When she sits down to watch those videos with us, we're all transformed, at least for the moment.

Memory is so vital to human beings. St. Augustine, who virtually invented the Western notion of the "self," believed that the core of our selves consists of our memories and the way that those memories continue to shape us. What is true personally is also true communally. My favorite definition of the church comes from an American theologian who calls it "a people of faith with a shared memory."

The words of Jesus at the Last Supper, "Do this in memory of me" formed the church's liturgy. In addition to keeping alive the memory of Jesus at each Eucharist, we have countless feast days throughout the year to remember the saints and heroes of our tradition—to call to mind those who have lived the faith before us in profound ways. We consecrate forty days of Lent to remember the life of Jesus, and finally, on Easter, his Resurrection. These memories shape who we are. These memories are etched into my being and I can join the psalmist in prayers of gratitude and praise for the marvels that the Lord has done. I can only hope that my children will, too.

Jack Richards is a photographer in Denver, Colorado.

SATURDAY OF THE SECOND WEEK OF LENT

"It is only right that we should celebrate and rejoice because your brother here was dead and has come to life; he was lost and is found."   Luke 15:32

I AM ONE OF THOSE CATHOLICS who was quite ignorant of what Lent meant when I was growing up.

I never went to Catholic school, except for one year in third grade in Hartford City, Indiana. The one thing I remember about that year was a pretty little girl with blonde bangs named Faith, who I was in love with.

My mother was Lutheran but my parents must have had an agreement about my brother and me being Catholics, because my father, only a casual Catholic himself, made sure we got to Mass on Sunday and observed those old Lenten regulations. My mother, who rarely went to her church, never objected.

I suffered through Lent then. I never did much in the way of sacrifice or penance. I used to stay up late on days of fast and abstinence just so I could have a ham sandwich and a cold glass of milk at one minute after midnight. Not the right attitude, I guess.

It was my wife who rescued me. She had been educated in Catholic schools until we met at a city college and got married during World War II. She taught me that Lent is a time of personal commitment to a penitential frame of mind, with emphasis on charitable works of mercy, added prayers and, ideally, daily Mass—the greatest prayer of all.

The aim, as we understand Lent today, is to grow in personal spirituality and grace, however we decide to do it.

We smile when we hear some of our fellow parishioners bemoan the loss of the old Lent—especially as they're coming out of daily Mass. We want to tell them but don't, that it's our choice now what we do for Lent. Follow the old Lenten regulations if you want; read spiritual books and magazines; pay more attention to your diocesan newspaper; take part in Lenten study programs; give your time and talents to parish Outreach programs, the local soup kitchen or hospital, a home for unwed mothers—whatever.

The church treats us as adults now. We need to act like it.

James A. Doyle served as the Executive Director of the Catholic Press Association from 1958–1988. His most recent book, Two Voices, *Liguori Press, 1996, was co-authored with his son, Brian Doyle.*

THIRD SUNDAY OF LENT

Year A   *John 4:5-42*

IN 1931, PEARL BUCK WAS AWARDED a Pulitzer Prize for her novel *The Good Earth*. She was also the first American woman to receive the Nobel Prize for Literature. Although it would appear that her literary contributions were among her greatest achievements, Pearl Buck prized her missionary work much more than her writing. Through her extensive travel, her study and her commitment to working with people from various cultures, the celebrated author made this important observation, *"The basic discovery about any people is the discovery of the relationships between its men and women."*

If Pearl Buck was right, we have to ask ourselves what discovery we can make about the world in which Jesus lived, and what then, can we discover about Jesus? The legal status of women in first century Israel excluded them from being credible witnesses in Jewish courts of law. Women were not permitted to read from the Torah or speak aloud during communal worship. They were considered to be a distraction to men engaged in prayer. And yet, throughout the gospels, we find that Jesus was unconcerned with the social norms that governed the relationships between men and women of his time. It would have been unheard of for a rabbi to engage in friendly conversation with a woman at a well, particularly a Samaritan woman. And yet, that is exactly what Jesus does.

Why does Jesus choose a Samaritan woman, married five times and living with a man to whom she is not married, to reveal the fact that he is the Messiah? It would seem that a conversation between a man and a woman distanced by race, gender, and religion held no promise. But in fact, Jesus recognized great potential in his relationship with the Samaritan woman, something that exceeded the limitations of their positions in life. This woman, rejected by society as an outcast, would bring the proclamation of the Good News to fulfillment.

Despite her social status and personal limitations, the Samaritan woman was open to hearing and responding to the Good News. The gospel tells us that many others came to faith as a result of her testimony. Could the same be said of the more righteous, the more socially accepted, the more powerful cast of characters found in the gospels? Could the same be said of us?

I don't know why the woman at the well was married five times, but I do know that the divorce laws of the day favored men. Perhaps she was infertile and could not produce an heir. Perhaps she was suffering in some other way. Jesus may have known something about the woman at the well that no one else knew. Maybe the Samaritan's secret left her more open to the Messianic secret and her wounded past opened her eyes and ears and heart in a way that nothing else could.

Because Jesus was a man, maleness became normative for certain rights and roles in arenas both secular and sacred. Unfortunately, this norm often resulted in the exclusion of women. Paradoxically, Jesus chose women to be his friends, his followers, and the first to proclaim the good news of the Resurrection. Jesus embraced humanity as a man, but the theological point is that he became human, not that he became male. All of us are called by grace to the same relationship with God that Jesus shared, regardless of our gender or role in society.

We live in a dualistic culture, as Jesus did, where the healthy integration of the masculine and the feminine sometimes escapes us. We're part of a society and part of a church where narrow gender roles can sometimes alienate us from one other, and therefore, alienate us from the truth of our humanity. Is it possible to think of a culture's journey or the journey of a faith community as one which is paralleled to our inner journey of conversion and wholeness? Perhaps, in this season of Lent, we can begin to heal both ourselves and the systems within which we try to love one another. Maybe it is only when we begin to reconcile the polarities within ourselves that we can begin to alleviate the same tensions that exist in the world around us.

In spite of the cultural norms that dictated life in first century Israel, Christ's relationships with women point to the truth that we are all made in the image of God and that the cultural standards that determine the relationships between men and women were, and perhaps still are, often perverse and unfaithful to the holiness of creation. The story of the Samaritan woman shows us that God's love for humanity is unconcerned with gender and power. Why then are we?

Year B   *John 2:13–25*

LIKE ANY GOOD CATHOLIC boy or girl, I could easily recite the core belief concerning the humanity of Jesus: He was like us in all things but sin. But there was always this nagging doubt about the sinlessness of Jesus lurking in the back of my young mind. Didn't Jesus drive the moneychangers out of the temple? He made a whip and chased out the animals and turned over tables of money lining the temple. He sounded angry to me. I was more than willing to forgive Jesus for his one venture into the world of human sinfulness, but the story made it hard for me to believe that Jesus was without sin.

The problem of course was in my own childish notions of sin. As far as I knew, anger was one of the seven deadly sins. So Jesus' anger must surely be a sin, right? Wrong. St. Augustine would say that it is sinful *not* to be angry in the face of injustice and evil. Jesus was angry that the temple had replaced worship with profit. The carnival atmosphere at the temple had little to do with the command to love God with all our heart, mind and soul. And so Jesus was angry, and rightly so.

On Ash Wednesday we are advised to repent or turn away from sin, and on the third Sunday of Lent we are encouraged to expand our notion of sin. Sin includes injustice in all its forms and if we're not part of the solution, then we're part of the problem. In Jesus' day, the prophetic act of Christ was to turn over the tables of the moneychangers. Today our prophets continue to fight injustice. Their lives give witness to the call to conversion, one that asks us to live for God's kingdom instead of our own. These prophets are hardly welcomed in our midst. We all seem to love and admire charity—direct care for the poor and needy. But we don't like to be reminded that we're part of the reason that the poor are poor. As Dorothy Day once said, "When I feed the poor, they call me a saint; when I ask why the poor are poor, they call me a communist." Conversion means more than conversion from my personal faults. It also involves conversion from comfort to a conviction and commitment to challenge social injustice as well.

Tony Marinelli is a teacher and author of several books including the award winning The Word Made Flesh *(Paulist Press, 1996).*

Year C   *Luke 13:1-9*

THERE ARE SOME WHO THINK that the three years that the fig tree produced no fruit is a reference to the three years of Jesus' public ministry, which failed to convince religious authorities that their ways were barren while the message of Jesus bore spiritual fruit. Jewish leaders wanted Jesus crucified and were themselves "cut down" with the fall of Jerusalem in 70A.D. Others think back to Leviticus 19, where the author makes reference to the fruit of trees that are forbidden to be eaten for the first three years. Only in the fourth year will the fruit be holy, and only in the fifth year are Jews allowed to eat of the fruit. Was it only after three years of public ministry, after his death and resurrection, that Jesus was understood to be the Messiah?

Jesus tells us that the owner of the barren fig tree wants the tree cut down, but the vinedresser promises to tend to it, hoping that it will eventually bear fruit. If it fails to bear fruit after that, the vinedresser agrees to cut it down.

Is it possible that the extra time and extra care is Lent and our Lenten observances? Are these the forty days that we have to reform, to pay attention to the ways in which we have failed to bear fruit? If we tend to our negligent ways, if we feed our spiritual selves through study and prayer, will we then bear the fruit of Easter? If we walk the way of Jesus, will we then share in the Resurrection? I hope so, but I hope so every year, every Lent, and yet I admit, the forty days speed by and conversion escapes me every year.

What makes this year different? I lost my twin brother in a terrible accident. He thought he had a lot of years ahead of him. We often talked about retiring and moving South where we could fish year round.

The story of the fig tree reminds me that I might not have as much time on this earth as I think I do. If I let Lent get by me again because I'm tied up with the business or demands of my job, is it possible that I'll be cut down, like the barren tree? Maybe my promise to make good next year won't work for God. Truth is, it doesn't work for me. So this year, my Lenten motto is: Now or Never, Bear Fruit or Be Cut Down.

Robert Pritchard grew up in a family whose business was trees. Today he is an attorney in New Jersey.

MONDAY OF THE THIRD WEEK OF LENT

"As the deer yearns for running streams, so I yearn for you, my God."   *Psalm 42:1*

ONE OF THE MOST BEAUTIFUL LINES in all the Lenten psalms begs the question: what does my soul long for? Can I join the psalmist in prayer and say in honesty that my soul longs for God? Or does my soul yearn for stuff; for comfort, ease, rest, happiness, wealth, security, and maybe a great vacation. Let's face it, many of us have anesthetized our souls. I sometimes feel as if I've made a pact with my culture, bought and sold myself for the American dream. If my soul yearned for God, wouldn't I live differently? Wouldn't I pray more, give more, learn more? Would I settle for the simple truth that I'm lucky to have been born in the right place and the right time? Would I plan differently for my children? Truth is I yearn for a 34 waist again. I yearn for a job with less aggravation, for a life with fewer problems. I can't remember the last time I yearned for God.

Lent is my chance to turn things around. This is the time to take another look at my life, my joys, my desires and my relationship with God. Maybe if I knew Him better, I'd yearn for Him more, as the lover yearns for his beloved.

Patrick O'Hare is a computer programmer in Raleigh, North Carolina.

TUESDAY OF THE THIRD WEEK OF LENT

"Direct me in your ways, Yahweh, and teach me your paths. Encourage me to walk in your truth and teach me since you are the God who saves me."

Psalm 25:4-5

THERE ARE A LOT OF THEORIES about Lent, which has been a Christian time of penitence and almsgiving since the fourth century. Perhaps the forty days are meant to reflect the forty days Moses spent on Mount Sinai or the forty years his people wandered in the desert or the forty days of the flood or the forty days Jesus spent fasting in the desert.

Perhaps Lenten fasting was created by the Catholic church in the 18th century to save the Portuguese fishing industry.

Although my children and I are episodic churchgoers and we range in faith from quasi-agnostic to quasi-Roman Catholic, in our own way we each observe Lent. I try to give up something or add something that, like a pebble in my shoe or a string around my finger, helps me remember whatever it is that Lent signifies—and reminds me to have faith. I have tried adding daily readings, doing service in soup kitchens and homeless shelters, going to church more often and tithing to the church, all with mixed success.

Last year I decided to give up saying the F-word and the S-word, two words I don't use in front of my children and that I don't want to hear them say, either. I thought this would be easy. It was almost impossible. At least once a day I found myself swearing at my computer screen, at a balking running shoe, at the telephone. Although I didn't change much, I was frequently reminded of my faith. This year I am trying to give up sugar, criticism in general and the word *but* in particular. No sugar, that's easy. No *buts*, that's hard. My 18-year-old daughter has given up chewing gum, as she did last year. This works well for her. Every time she wants a piece of gum—and that's dozens of times a day—she thinks of Jesus and the Easter story.

My son wanted to give up vegetables last year, but I wouldn't let him. Instead he decided to give up fruit. I was about to tell him that giving up something healthful wasn't appropriate. Then I thought twice. I believe that the most precious thing I can give my children, more precious than good eating or even good friends, is some kind of faith in some kind of higher order. Although I can't guarantee this for them—only God can do that—I think I can put them in the way of God's grace. Whether they end up as Buddhists or Baptists, Quakers or Catholics, I hope they will find a faith that sustains them, and some way to observe faith. Faith is the big thing; broccoli is a small thing. I said my son could give up fruit. Now he's given up vegetables. Next year he plans to give up soap. I say we'll talk about that after Easter.

Susan Cheever, daughter of writer John Cheever, is the author of ten books and a weekly column syndicated throughout the United States.

WEDNESDAY OF THE THIRD WEEK OF LENT

"Praise Yahweh, O Jerusalem, Zion, praise your God."   **Psalm 147:12**

In Church At Lent

An old woman
Has two daughters
Or nieces or
Neighboring girls.

They are not young,
The young women:
Maybe fifty
Each, maybe twins.

The mom reaches
Up to brush back
Their gleaming hoods
As Mass is born.

The two girls stare
At the woman
A tick too long
And I see that

Something is off:
They are too calm.
The girls hold hands
All during Mass,

And look at their
Mother or aunt
Or neighbor lady,
Whomever she is,

For when to kneel,
When to stand, when
To cup their hands
For the sweet bread

In this stark time
The mother is calm.
Her face is taut
Her hair stone gray,

Her gestures deft
With her placid
Silent children.
When Mass ends they

Face the mother
Whose patient hand
Flips their bright hoods
Up again. They stand

And holding hands
Still, follow her
Blankly smiling
Into gleaming rain.

Brian Doyle is the editor of Portland, *the University of Portland magazine. He is the author of* Thoughts of Home, *Hearst Books, 1995, and* Two Voices, *which Brian co-authored with his father, James Doyle. Brian lives in Oregon with his wife and three children.*

THURSDAY OF THE THIRD WEEK OF LENT
"Do not harden your hearts."   *Psalm 95:8*

MY KID BROTHER JOE was always a jerk. He was a wiseguy and usually in trouble. I was the dutiful son; honor rolls, dean's lists, law review. Joe got married just after his twentieth birthday and nine months later, he and his wife had their first child. I was in my second year of law school in California.

I flew home for the christening to see his son and my nephew for the first time. When I walked into his house, my brother and his wife were standing in the kitchen with their son. Joe saw me and smiled. I walked over, kissed his wife, looked at his son and began to weep. I hugged my surprised brother and told him how happy I was for him. I quickly found my way to the bathroom, closed the door, and cried like a baby. What seemed to be tears of joy were not. Three months earlier, my girlfriend and I had decided we were not ready for a baby (or marriage) and she ended the pregnancy quickly. We had convinced ourselves that "it was best for everyone." In those three months I had managed to build a wall around my heart strong enough to keep the truth about what we had done far from my conscience.

Today, I thank God for the gift of my nephew in ways that he will never know. It took nothing less than his beautiful, miraculous face to soften my hardened heart. That's not to say it stayed that way. I still find myself building walls to keep myself from the truth of my life or the life around me; the hungry, the imprisoned, the poor. I wonder sometimes if the Pharisees had hardened their hearts. Did Judas harden his heart in order to betray his friend? The stories found in the Lenten readings always call me to conversion, the breaking down of my hardened heart.

Peter Hartnett is an attorney in Nevada.

FRIDAY OF THE THIRD WEEK OF LENT

"You must love the Lord your God with all your heart, with all your soul, with all your mind and with all your strength." Mark 12:30

FOR AN ITINERANT PREACHER with calloused hands, dusty feet, and no extensive education in the law, Jesus really knew his Torah. He knew his Father, and no amount of trickery from religious leaders could overcome the sure knowledge that flowed from his deep unity with the author of all law.

In Mark 12, the evangelist records several of these devious attempts by the hierarchy of the day to ensnare him in his own words. The question in today's reading came from a scribe who appeared to be asking out of a less malignant spirit. All he wanted was for Jesus to name the chief commandment of the more than 600 that guided Jewish life. It was not necessarily a trap, but an invitation to serious reflection.

Like the pious and observant Jew that he was, Jesus started with the Shema, the world-shattering monotheistic insight of the Jewish people, reported in Deuteronomy. "Hear, O Israel; the Lord our God, the Lord is one; you shall love the Lord your God with all your heart, and with all your soul, and with all your mind, and with all your strength."

Seamlessly, he followed that with a reference to the more human-centered command from Leviticus—in effect, knitting the two commands together into one overwhelming rule of life. "The second is this, 'You shall love your neighbor as yourself.' There is no commandment greater than these."

These are not just the law of the Old Testament, but a summary of the character of Jesus himself. Two central keys to understanding Jesus, our great brother, lie in his absolute obsession with God and God's reign, and in his self-emptying. Call him God-obsessed, God-driven, God-filled. It comes down to this: Throughout his life, Jesus always chose God's reign over any other consideration, including his own physical safety. The Agony in the Garden gives evidence that these choices were not always easy, but for the God-driven rabbi from Nazareth, no choice but God's reign rang true.

Both in his relationship with the Father and his dealings with people, Jesus acted out of a deep *kenosis*, the Greek word for self-emptying. It means service to others, putting the needs of others ahead of your own needs. It means loving others in the same way as you love yourself, wanting for them what's necessary to live and be well. So the answer that Jesus gave to the scribe does more than sum up the law. It sums up the God-obsessed, self-emptying nature of the one we seek to emulate, especially in Lent, the season leading up to the greatest act of self-emptying: obedience even to death on the cross.

His answer, offered at a time when his critics were always ready to test him, gives us a test to use on ourselves this Lent and always: Are we obsessed with God? Can we truly be called self-emptying?

Bob Keeler is the author of Parish Alive!. *He won a Pulitzer prize in 1996 and in 2001 co-authored* Days of Intense Emotion: Praying with Pope John Paul II *in the Holy Land (Resurrection Press).*

SATURDAY OF THE THIRD WEEK OF LENT

"Have mercy on me, O God, in your faithful love, in your great tenderness wipe away my offenses."

Psalm 51:1

REPENTANCE IS A RELIGIOUS CONCERN for all faiths. Muslims pilgrimage to Mecca or maintain penitential rituals throughout the month of Ramadan. Millions of Hindus bathe away their sins in the Ganges River. Every Jew hopes to go to the Western Wall in Jerusalem at least once in his or her lifetime and until then, honors Yom Kippur through prayer and fasting and an examination of conscience and action. In the year 2000, twenty-five million

Christians traveled to Rome to celebrate the Jubilee Year of forgiveness. But even more Christians enter into Lent every year for forty days of prayer, fasting and almsgiving, all aimed at repentance for past sins and conversion that leads to new life.

But do rituals and religious practices themselves bring God's forgiveness and a change of heart? I don't think so. It's what those rites and prayers and sacrifices make of us. They're designed to change us, to focus us, to keep us mindful of our relationship to God and others, and our responsibility to act justly and love compassionately in light of those relationships.

When I ask God's forgiveness, when I ask forgiveness of my spouse or a colleague or my children, it has to be with the promise to try harder to live with more awareness of who I am in relationship to God and all creation. And that, for me, is always the hardest part of saying I'm sorry—knowing that an awful lot of work has to follow those words.

Ann Pizzano is a marketing analyst living in Westchester and working in Manhattan. She and two of her colleagues use their morning commute to pray the psalms and read through the gospels.

FOURTH SUNDAY IN LENT

YEAR A   *John 9:1–41*

AS MY GRANDMOTHER reached the end of her long life, she began to lose her sight. Her blindness went through progressively worsening stages until, at the end, she could only recognize the strongest contrasts of light and dark.

A parallel process took place in her mind. As she lost her sight, she increasingly lost contact with the world around her and began to live more in a totally private world of memory, fantasy, and imagination. She frequently could not remember where she was and often could not distinguish between what had happened in her dreams and what was actual. The things that were most important to her remained clear: she recognized her family and her relationship to them. All the rest—time and place and circumstance—became as blurred and indistinct as her vision.

This Lenten gospel presents us with a similar parallel between physical sight and mind. Sight is used symbolically as a metaphor concerning spiritual insight or faith. The blind man in the story gains both his physical sight and spiritual insight about Jesus. He comes to see physically in a single symbolic gesture of washing; but this is only the beginning of his journey towards faith. At first he identifies his healer simply as "the man called Jesus." Then he acknowledges him as a prophet. Still later he claims that Jesus must be from God. And at last his spiritual eyes are fully opened in the final encounter with Jesus who reveals himself as the Son of Man.

At the same time, the Pharisees grow progressively blinder. Initially, they are open to the blind man's miraculous healing; but subsequently their minds begin to close: they begin to doubt the man and call upon his parents. In anger and frustration they vilify the witness and throw him out. Finally, their refusal to believe is judged by Jesus as spiritual blindness.

The church traditionally connects this passage with baptism. The blind man's washing, which brings sight and begins the process that culminates in acknowledging Jesus, symbolizes the sacrament of initiation into the faith community. This gospel reading was especially appropriate for Lent, during which catechumens were prepared for baptism at the Easter Vigil (a practice now restored in the Rite of Christian Initiation for Adults). Their eyes are to be opened to a new vision of faith through their decision to respond to Christ, the light.

For those who are long-standing members of the community, particularly those who were baptized as infants and received its teachings as a part of their familial heritage, the emphasis on human choice in the conclusion of the gospel passage is an important reminder. Being a Christian is essentially a matter of making a free decision for faith in Jesus and all that it implies. It means choosing to see spiritually, to judge things in the light of Jesus' example and teaching. This gospel reminds us that unlike physical sight, spiritual insight is something about which we have a choice and for which we are responsible. We are still in the process symbolized by the blind man: gaining the vision that began when we entered the faith community through baptism, learning just who the Son of Man is and how we are to relate to him. Lent is an invitation to renew our decision to see clearly, to live by the light of faith that we have been given.

Richard Viladesau, S.T.D. is a professor of Theology at Fordham University and author or several books including The Word in and Out of Season *(Paulist Press, 1992).*

YEAR B *John 3:14–21*

THE LENTEN SEASON BEGINS with ashes and repentance and ends with crucifixion and death. Lent is preparation for Easter. If Easter is a celebration of victory over death, then Lent tells us something about how that happens. My childhood notions of Lent were focused on the importance of sacrifice and self-mortification—"giving stuff up." But I didn't understand then that "giving stuff up" really was an attempt to train me in the art of moving beyond my satisfaction with creaturely comforts and my own isolated ego and self. Lent is about repentance, but it's a life-giving repentance. If Lent is a journey from ashes to Easter, the old self must die, and the new self, rooted in Christ and in God must live. What I have come to realize with the passage of time, is that Easter begins not at the moment of physical death, but at the moment of genuine conversion, which is always a spiritual death. Every time I move closer to God's love, I am "raised up," I enter more fully into a relationship that cannot die, that knows no tomb.

Jesus tells Nicodemus that whoever believes in him will not die but have eternal life.

In order to believe this we must give new meaning to the word "die," because with certainty, we'll all die. But death will not be the last word. God's love is the last Word and the first Word and all words in between.

Tony Marinelli has been teaching high school religion to teenagers on Long Island for 23 years.

YEAR C *Luke 15:11-32*

I LEFT HOME IN 1977. With college behind me and the world before me, I turned my back on New York and set my sights on Atlanta. I barely noticed my parents' disappointment, their sighs and sad looks. After all, birds had to fly and fish had to swim. And wasn't it God who told Abram to *"Go forth from the land of your kinsfolk and from your father's house to a land that I will show you."*

And so I left. I found a great job, a great apartment, and discovered the many meanings of southern comfort. I ate barbecue, drank bourbon, and fell in love with a Baptist from Alabama. Life south of the Mason-Dixon line sure was sweet.

I called home regularly. Every once in a while Mom would ask a question like, "What's the name of your parish down there?" I'd mumble something about Saint Scarlett and quickly change the subject. The truth was I hadn't found the Catholic church in Atlanta yet. Probably because I hadn't looked.

I was busy, busy doing a lot of things, but most importantly, I was separating. I had left family and friends and all that was familiar to journey toward adulthood, a journey that would take me far from the childhood I had loved.

The South surprised me with a promotion at work and a proposal of marriage. Getting married was not high on my list of things to do that year, but I did agree to meet his parents if he would agree to slow down a little. We made a deal and drove deep into Dixie to meet the folks. They were wonderful people and things went just fine, until my prospective in-laws casually mentioned that they would never attend a wedding held in a Catholic church. I suddenly felt like a stranger in a strange land.

In Hebrew, the literal translation for conversion or *repentance is "coming to one's senses," feeling an impulse to return, to retrace one's steps and go home.*

I wanted to go home. Like the prodigal son, I left family and, perhaps faith, to explore the unknown. He strayed and squandered; he lived singly and selfishly. So did I. But somewhere in the sin that separates lies the grace that forgives, that heals and strengthens; a grace that instructs folly with wisdom and finds what has been lost. I missed my family. I missed my friends. And I missed who I had been. By year's end, I knew it was time to bid the Bible Belt goodbye.

My homecoming was heralded with warm welcomes all around. I arrived within a week of my best friend's wedding. When we gathered at the church for the ceremony, I was immediately soothed by the song and symbols that had formed the religious imagination of my youth. The words of the gospel were as familiar as the fairy tales that once lulled me to sleep. The voice and vision of Christ welcomed me with open arms. I knew where I was and who I was. I was Catholic and I was home.

In his poem "Little Gidding," T.S. Eliot said,

> We shall not cease from exploration
> And the end of all exploring

Will be to arrive where we started
And know the place for the first time.
When the last of earth left to discover
Is that which was the beginning.

Catholicism was my beginning, it was who I was in my marrow bone. It was what I celebrated and how I celebrated, a language I spoke and understood. The sounds and scents, the silence and celebration, all were part of me. Perhaps distance had helped bring that into focus. Returning home allowed me to claim the communion, the closeness, and the Christianity that once claimed me.

The prodigal son returned home with a new understanding of who he was, who his father was, and perhaps, who God was. Could it be that my journey had really been a pilgrimage, human life moving toward the divine? Maybe our real home is neither north nor south, nor here nor there, but with God and a community that sees and thinks and speaks as we do. My journey of faith included a detour through the deep south that in its end, brought me home. And I've never looked back.

MONDAY OF THE FOURTH WEEK OF LENT

"You have turned my mourning into dancing, you have stripped off my sackcloth and clothed me with joy. So my heart will sing to you unceasingly, Yahweh, my God, I shall praise you forever."

Psalm 30:11-12

LENT IS A SEASON which should mean a great deal to Catholics. Each year, as I write my pastorals to our people,

I recall the example of Jesus in his forty days and nights of prayer and fasting in the wilderness. From what Jesus did and taught we learn as well: Lent is a season for our prayer, our penance, and our almsgiving. Part of my own Lenten observance, for many years, is to try to pray each day the Way of the Cross, using the traditional stations as a basis for meditation. For this, I have been blessed with two kinds of visual helps. In my chapel is a silver circle in which are represented the individual Stations of the Cross. Most Lenten weekdays, I use this to follow Jesus on his way from condemnation to Calvary.

Also in my house, thanks to the goodness of an Italian classmate during days of graduate studies in Rome, there are depictions of the fourteen stations in a modern style. Both the pastor and I find these challenging, thought-provoking, prayer-sustaining images. The vivid red of the blood of Jesus, the drama of the crucifixion, with darkness covering the earth, and the pathos of our Blessed Lady, a witness to it all, truly touch the heart.

In addition, I encourage our people to walk with me in making Lenten Fridays not only days of abstinence but also days of fast before the Lord.

Finally, each day must have its special time of prayer. I find that the daily readings for the celebration of the Eucharist are most helpful in offering themes for meditation, to help us walk more closely with Jesus as he goes up to Jerusalem for those days of suffering and of glory. This, with the Rosary and the celebration of Mass complete my Lenten program.

Lent is a time of almsgiving, and one can find many good causes asking for help. Our own annual Lenten Appeal and the works of CRS have a special claim on me.

Please God, Lent observed in this way prepares both head and heart for a joyous Easter celebration, when we are reminded of the power of the Lord Jesus to re-fire not only our hope but the fabric of our lives themselves.

Cardinal William H. Keeler, Archdiocese of Baltimore

TUESDAY OF THE FOURTH WEEK OF LENT

"God is both refuge and strength for us, a help always ready in trouble; so we shall not be afraid."

Psalm 46:1-2

WHEN I WAS YOUNGER, Lent was always a difficult time and a true test of my will power. I think that's because life was so easy and uncomplicated back then. Today, life seems more difficult, and rather than dread the forty days of Lent, I look forward to them. They are, in a way, my refuge from a trying job, an overcrowded schedule and uncertain times.

I work in lower Manhattan. I was on the roof of my office building when the second plane hit the Tower. I was never so scared as I was at that moment. While others around me grabbed cameras and reached for their cell phones, I stood frozen in prayer. I remember thinking that in these times, God is our only refuge. God is also our strength. Millions of Americans, joined by people all around the world, flocked to churches and synagogues that night. It was clear to human beings from all corners of the earth that God is our refuge and our strength and God's people will be responsible for becoming the refuge and strength of the world.

I look forward to Lent because my parish always sponsors a week long retreat for families. Not only do my wife and I look forward to it, now my young adult children look forward to it, as well.

It's as if they've come to a realization of how important God is in their lives sooner than we did because they will raise their children in a different world, a more frightening world than my generation ever could have imagined.

I've noticed more people attending noon Mass at Lent in lower Manhattan than in years gone by. I feel strengthened by their prayers and presence, fortified by their signs of peace. I feel strength in our numbers, in the unity of the Body of Christ. For a time, every day after Mass, I am reminded of the words of the 46th psalm: we shall not be afraid. And I'm not.

Stan Lupski is an engineer and a daily communicant in New York.

WEDNESDAY OF THE FOURTH WEEK OF LENT

"Can a mother forget her baby at the breast, feel no pity for the child she has born? Even if these were to forget, I shall not forget you." Isaiah 49:15

SEEMS TO ME THAT LENT, like motherhood, comes with a grace of its own. I didn't always believe that. Growing up I thought Lent was like going to the doctor to get a shot that felt awful, but was good for me. Now I think Lent, in itself, is good for me because with these forty days come a certain grace. Maybe it's the grace of transformation, a call to become, as St. Paul says, "a new creation." I only know that I'm carried through Lent every year by someone or something other than myself. Not unlike my call to motherhood. There are days when I don't know how I'll get from morning to night. But I do. And at the end of the toughest days, I feel a certain peace, or grace, or closeness with God. It's as if God draws nearer to us when our lives are stretched and our hearts are tested.

During Lent, I'm more focused on my faith, more attentive to the readings at Mass, more drawn to the Eucharist than I usually am. I seem to be more unselfish and conscious of others, more willing to make sacrifices, not for the sake of sacrifice, but for the desire to share the grace that has fallen on me. What could it be other than Lenten grace that changes me so profoundly? What could it be other than the grace of motherhood that allows me to understand why Isaiah compares God's love for us to a mother's love?

Marly Becker is an architect in Arizona and the mother of a little girl named Grace.

THURSDAY OF THE FOURTH WEEK OF LENT

"You pore over the scriptures, believing that in them you can find eternal life."　　　　　　　　*John 5:39*

WHEN I WAS A YOUNG SEMINARIAN, way back before Vatican II, I liked Lent because of the weekday Mass readings. In those days, the weekday readings throughout most of the year were generally pretty uninteresting. There were sets of readings for Masses for the dead, and for the various classes of saints whose feasts occurred throughout the year, but they were always the same. Many people who went to daily Mass knew most of the Mass readings by heart, and nobody paid much attention to them.

But Lent was special! Here we had different readings for every single day, and not just New Testament readings. We heard from people that were strangers to us for most of the rest of the year: Joel and Jeremiah and Isaiah. There was even a little mystery story from the book of Daniel about a beautiful girl named Susanna and the elders. If nothing else there was variety, and, although Lent was always primarily a season to fast, the liturgy readings gave us a daily chance to feast.

After the Council, the general situation changed. In response to the directives of The Constitution on the Sacred Liturgy (no. 51),the treasures of the Bible were opened up "more lavishly." Now there were different readings not just for the weekdays of Lent, but for every weekday throughout the year. Catholics who went to daily Mass began to be nourished by a much greater variety of scriptural food.

The weekday readings for Lent in the new Lectionary are slightly different from the former ones, but I continue to be grateful for them. There are three basic themes in these readings, themes that are intertwined and that keep us aware of what Lent is all about. The readings call each of us to repentance, to a change of heart. They also keep us aware (especially in the fourth and fifth weeks) that this is the season of final preparation for baptism on the part of the Church's catechumens and so offer the basics of Jesus' teaching. Thirdly, as Lent draws to its climax, the readings recall the tensions and controversies that led to Jesus' death and so prepare us to celebrate Holy Week.

A few years ago I wrote a little book on the weekday readings of Lent. It was based on the brief impromptu homilies that I preached at the noon Mass at the downtown church where I live. I called it *Lenten Lunches*. The title suggested that what was offered was not intended to be a substantial treatment of the readings, but only a quick snack in a time of fasting. I suppose I would give the book the same title if I were writing it again.

But if I ever got a chance to do real justice to the Lenten weekday readings, to reflect on and set forth the deeper richness and nourishment that they contain, I would need a different title. Instead of *Lenten Lunches*, I might call it *Banquets for a Fasting People*.

In any case, I am grateful for the Vatican II Lectionary, grateful for the weekday readings of Lent, and grateful for the way the Lord's word nourishes its people.

Most Rev. Daniel E. Pilarczyk, Archbishop of Cincinnati

FRIDAY OF THE FOURTH WEEK OF LENT

"Yahweh is near to the broken-hearted, he helps those whose spirits have been crushed."　　　　**Psalm 34:18**

"RELIGION," KARL MARX TELLS US, "is the opium of the masses." Marx examined the society in which he lived and concluded that religion helps the poor remain poor. Like a drug, it gives temporary solace while it sets their sights on heaven—instead of helping them here on earth. The Marxist critique of religion has been joined by psychological and philosophical critiques that proclaim God to be a projection of human need for eternal significance. God didn't create us—we created God to fill the void of human mortality and insignificance, they say. For Marx and Freud and others like them, the idea that Yahweh is near to the broken-hearted is an illusion to which inadequate personalities cling.

But the biblical insight reminds us that God is near to those who hurt. This is not meant as a cosmic pacifier, but rather a theological, psychological, and moral truth. To say that God is near to the broken-hearted tells us something about God. Our Creator is a living God who remains close to his creation through love and mercy and compassion. Jesus knew this. He called God Abba, a father who held his poor, hungry, sick and suffering children close to him.

The broken-hearted sometimes know something that the comfortable and the bloated will never know: on the other side of suffering is a redemptive love that draws us more deeply into our humanity and into God's love. Victor Frankl knew it. He was a young psychiatrist in Vienna who had studied Freudian psychology and was left cold by it. His experience of profound suffering in four different concentration camps convinced him that suffering and meaning can go hand in hand. The love that human beings are capable of is a suffering, self-surrendering love. Being broken-hearted can move us toward a spirituality rooted in love and solidarity with the poor. Protected hearts might never know that. Oscar Wilde's story of *The Happy Prince* reminds us that even those of us who are protected by wealth, isolated by it, really, can discover happiness through compassion for those less fortunate. The prince's heart is broken and redeemed.

The psalmist can teach us a profound moral lesson. If God is near to the broken-hearted, we are called to be near to them as well. The church, as the body of Christ in the world, is bound by the command of Jesus to love one another as he loves us. That love was one that reached out to the broken and the marginal. At the heart of the church must be a mission of service to those most in need. Contrary to the Marxist critique of religion, Christian faith is meant to challenge us to stand with those who are most in need. Maybe the penitential season of Lent can inspire me to reflect on the question of whether or not I have been open and responsive to the broken-hearted, as God is.

Sheila Lenihan lives in Minneapolis, where she is a wife, mother, and school nurse.

SATURDAY OF THE FOURTH WEEK OF LENT

"God is a shield that protects me, saving the honest of heart."   **Psalm 7:10**

I THINK OFTEN ABOUT GOD'S PROMISE to His people. We are His and He is ours. My question is always, "are we worthy of His protection, His promise of mercy and compassionate love?"

I was shipped to Vietnam when I was 19 years old. On the morning we were scheduled to leave, the chaplain, whose name I can't even remember, said some words that changed my life. He said, "God will be your shield in battle. I thought about that a lot in Vietnam and it always gave me a feeling of safety. I took some chances that may have saved my life. Who knows if I would have made the same decisions if God's protection was not part of my thinking.

Today, I face a different battle—colon cancer. When the chaplain in the hospital came in to see me the morning of my surgery, he promised God's protection throughout the operation. My mind rushed back thirty years. Again, I entered the battlefield, this time it was an operating room, filled with a feeling that God was present and His will would again be done.

Well, I'm still here, thankful for the chaplain, whose name I can't remember, but whose words are unforgotten.

Tim Sheridan is a retired policeman living outside of Philadelphia, Pennsylvania.

FIFTH SUNDAY OF LENT
YEAR A *John 11:1–45*

WHEN JESUS ARRIVES IN BETHANY he is faced with an agonizing event. Lazarus has been defeated by the final experience of human limitation—death. Mary and Martha are grieving and Jesus himself is moved to tears. We gain remarkable insight here into a God who cries, who weeps with us because he is so intimately involved with our humanity.

Jesus directs those surrounding the cave to "take the stone away." He calls Lazarus out of the tomb and then tells the unbelieving bystanders to "unbind him, let him go free." Could the manner in which Jesus raises Lazarus from the dead be significant? Surely Jesus could have removed the stone or loosened the linen strips that kept Lazarus bound. But he doesn't. He invites others to participate in this lifegiving event. He asks the community to help Lazarus conquer the experience of death, to free him of his bonds, and help him walk away from his tomb. I suspect that he asks the same of us two thousand years later. He directs us to call each other out of the darkness of sin and injustice, or maybe the darkness of addiction or imprisonment. Today's gospel suggests that we lead each other to the light of resurrection.

God asks our help in making the experience of resurrection a reality in each other's lives. We're the ones who do the work of rolling away stones and loosening ties. We're the ones who wipe away tears and speak words of consolation in times of turmoil. We call each other out of our tombs through experiences of love, intimacy and affirmation. The story of Lazarus is a story of overcoming our limitations through a faith nourished within a community of believers. Perhaps that's the only way that we can ever hope to understand the resurrection.

YEAR B *John 12:20–33*

CATHOLIC THEOLOGY HAS TRADITIONALLY USED philosophy as her most able assistant in trying to understand the mysteries of faith. Today, it seems that psychology has made its claim in helping us to understand the role of theology in our lives. Psychology can help affirm the ancient wisdom of the church, but theology can also learn from psychology. The Second Vatican Council affirmed the legitimate role of the sciences in helping all humanity, including the church, arrive at a deeper and broader understanding of what it means to be human.

On this day in Lent, Jesus tells his apostles that "unless a grain of wheat falls into the earth and dies, it remains only a single grain; but if it dies, it yields a rich harvest." Theologically, the Gospel of John is referring to the death and resurrection of Jesus. But psychologically, Jesus is talking about the process of human transformation and growth.

I am reminded of Erik Erikson's description of the eight stages of human life. In order to go from one stage to the next, a certain "dying" is required. The infant leaves the security of the womb to venture into the unknown. A toddler must assert his independence and die to absolute dependency in order to move away from his parents (physically and emotionally) and develop a healthy ego. The young child takes risks and initiative with others in order to expand his or her own self and knowledge of the world. The school age child dies to the security of the home and rises to new self-confidence in the world of teachers and peers. Adolescents die to many childhood certainties and attachments in order to establish their own identities. Young adults die to the self-absorption of adolescence in order to enter into mature and intimate relationships. Adults must die to their romantic gazes and personal interests in order to nurture and develop the next generation. And when we've reached a certain age, hopefully we have died and been raised so many times that our old age is filled with wisdom and a sense of purpose and meaning to life. A failure to be willing to die at each stage of life breeds, not transformation, but, in the words of Erikson: distrust, shame, guilt, inferiority, identity confusion, isolation, stagnation and despair.

The dying that Jesus refers to is a dying of a smaller self for the birth of a larger self. Erikson thinks in the same terms when talking about human development. In Christian spirituality, it means dying to all that keeps us from loving God and each other as deeply and as fully as we can, and it means rising to new life in Christ. With each "death," there is a resurrection, a moving more fully into the mystery of God's love.

Perhaps St. Irenaeus captured the union of psychology and spirituality best when he said, "The glory of God is a human being fully alive—and the glory of the human person is the vision of God." Nature and grace are the most intimate of partners.

YEAR C   *John 8:1-11*

THE MORE THINGS CHANGE, the more they stay the same. I recently saw a movie about Matthew Shepherd, the young man murdered because he was gay. Outside the church, people stood with banners and signs that declared that God hates fags and that Matthew burns in hell. Most, if not all of the people holding those signs call themselves Christian. Matthew's father, however, seemed to know something about Christianity that the hate mongers did not. He asked that his son's killers not be given the death penalty. Somewhere in his heart he could find mercy even when surrounded by the merciless. Obviously, the sign holders don't speak for their churches and clearly don't represent the majority of Christian people. And yet they claim hatred for homosexuals in God's name.

I love scripture. If I was stranded on a desert island and could have only one book, it would be the Bible. It provides such strength, clear guidelines and a positive direction for our lives. And yet, the Bible is often used as a tool for intolerance and hatred. Throughout the history of the church, the Bible has inspired saints and mystics, but it has also inspired Crusaders and Inquisitors. We have used the Bible to reach out to the poor and we've used it for anti-Semitism and blatant sexism.

The Catholic Church may be as guilty as any other church in these regards. But we're committed to the idea that the Bible is not to be read literally or taken completely at face value in every circumstance and situation. Christianity is a community of believers rooted in Christ. He is our Word. It is in and through Christ and the Spirit that we seek to read scripture and apply it to our lives today. Sometimes, we may have to conclude that what was written in a section of the Bible is a reflection of the limitations of the human author. For example, Deuteronomy commands that married women who commit adultery should be stoned to death. And Leviticus suggests that the same be done to those who commit homosexual acts. Do we really believe that these commands represent the universal will of God forever? No we don't. Nor do we accept the idea that wives must be submissive to their husbands or that the universe was created in six 24-hour days.

The story of the adulterous woman suggests that killing the sinner is not necessarily the solution to the problem of human sin. Jesus suggests mercy, love, compassion and justice. There's an enigmatic scene within the story of the adulterous woman. Jesus is sitting on the ground, writing in the dirt. We've never known what he wrote. This is my guess: he was writing the words of Jeremiah: "I will take away their hearts of stone and give to them hearts of flesh."

For me, Lent always begs God's forgiveness for the hatred in my heart, the need to retaliate and look down on others who have chosen sins different from my own. I'm comfortable with my sins, more tolerant of my mistakes than the shortcomings of others. If God could crush my stony heart this Lent, I'd live in the light of the Resurrection, not only on Easter, but every day, and those around me would know it.

Matthew King works as a high school chaplain in Nebraska.

MONDAY OF THE FIFTH WEEK OF LENT

"Yahweh is my shepherd, I lack nothing."   Psalm 23:1

MY BIRTHDAY IS IN MARCH, so it usually falls somewhere in the forty days of Lent. About a week or two before my birthday, my son or daughter will ask, "Mom, what do you want most for your birthday?"

Lent is a good time to think about what we want most, what we really need and what we want to become. If Yahweh is my shepherd, I already have everything I need and want. Right? Then why is it that I want to go to Hawaii and I want a bigger house. I want more time to myself and I want to lose 20 pounds. What does that say about me?

The Lenten gospels give us a beautiful account of Jesus' life, his teachings and an insight into his relationship with God. I guess that's the stuff I should be thinking about when I'm asked what I really want. Do I want to know more about Jesus? Do I want a closer relationship with him? Do I want to care for the least of my brothers and sisters more than I want a trip to Hawaii?

Lent is about dying to achieve new life. I certainly feel as if my years are numbered and the reality of death is no longer as remote as it used to be. I try to spend time in prayer; I attend a scripture reading group once a week in my parish; I give generously to charity. But I still feel as if I've got a long way to go in my spiritual life.

What do I want for my birthday? I want to fall asleep in God's arms, like an infant in its parents' arms, so content, that it falls deep asleep. If I had that, I think I could forgo the trip to Hawaii.

Dolores Zawicki is a beautician living in Louisiana.

TUESDAY OF THE FIFTH WEEK OF LENT
"Many came to believe in him."   John 8:30

MY FRIEND DON struggled more than anyone I know to find faith. Don, a retired New York City police sergeant, spent much of his free time reading lengthy and usually difficult theological tomes in hope of discovering answers. He didn't read apologists, either; Don wanted writers who inquired freely. Hans Kung, Edward Schillebeeckx and Teilhard de Chardin were among his favorites.

How, he wondered, could a man also be God? On many a summer night, we would sit out in our adjacent Brooklyn backyards and try to figure it out. Don made clear that he had little use for the institutional church, which seemed only to want to silence the writers he deemed most honest. So I was surprised one Sunday morning to find him at Mass, standing in the back of the church. We were at the 8 o'clock Mass—a rarity for me, a 10 o'clocker. It turned out he had been "darkening the door" (as he put it) at the 8 o'clock Mass for a while, figuring he wouldn't be seen there. His quest for the truth had led him into a church, despite his reservations about organized religion.

After Don became ill with lung cancer, it was difficult for him to go to Mass. I brought the Eucharist to him, and we would have a short service at his dining room table each Sunday afternoon. Don remarked on one of those occasions that he wondered how God could accept someone like him, a man who had such difficulty in believing. My eyes welled up. Don, I told him, I think that God must have a special love for you, because *you've tried so hard.*

Don died about two weeks later. There are mysteries here beyond my understanding, but I do believe that Don "came to believe in him" and that he is with the saints.

Paul Moses teaches journalism at Brooklyn College and is the co-author of Days of Intense Emotion: Praying with Pope John Paul II in the Holy Land *(Resurrection Press, 2001).*

WEDNESDAY OF THE FIFTH WEEK OF LENT

"If you make my word your home, you will indeed be my disciples; you will come to know the truth, and the truth will set you free."   John 8:31–32

DURING ONE OF THE DARKEST TIMES in my life, I found myself relating to a poster that adorned a door in a weekly meeting place. It depicted an old-fashioned wringer-washing machine; what was being wrung was a rag doll. She was halfway through her ordeal. "The truth will set you free," the text above the picture promised—such a comforting thought, only to be followed by the revelation of the text below: " . . . but first it will make you miserable."

How lucky I was to have been led to that place, to the support that was available as I desperately sought to discern what was true and what was not true in my own personal universe, and to find the faith to believe that Truth even existed. At that time, being confronted with the truth about the path to truth was strangely comforting. My very life was being wrung out of me. But knowing that a new life, and freedom, awaited me if I embraced the process gave purpose to my suffering. I sought the truth in all things, no matter what the cost. It cost everything, and my life has been restored a hundredfold.

That particular battle took many years, and many new challenges have come along to challenge the serenity and even sanity that have been the greatest rewards for the labor. Today, I find myself moving through Lent with breast cancer as my adversary. I am overwhelmed with gratitude that it was discovered and that I am being treated by wonderful professionals who are not only knowledgeable but caring, and I cannot describe the love and prayers that have surrounded me since the diagnosis. The tumor and the malignancies in the nodes were growing voraciously during a year when I thought all was well, health-wise. Had I not been faced with the mammogram and had I not then faced the diagnosis and pursued treatment, the *truth* is that I would still have cancer, it would be spreading through my whole body, and my days would surely be fewer in number than I thought. My days are all in God's hands, and I intend to live each one I am granted. The truth of any matter, no matter how dreadful, is the beginning of new life.

Since I really do know first-hand about God's unfailing graciousness, it is doubly distressing to know that I am still assaulted by my own character flaws and subject to anxiety and depression about my inadequacies. At times the real or perceived worries about something—from the state of the world and the church, to the sanctity of relationships, to the ability to *know the truth* and to maintain the commitment to bear with it—threaten to drown me in despair. It is then that I remember to become a disciple again. I am Peter, not walking on the water as invited and intended, but drowning in the wind and wild waters. My

Lenten preparation always includes the fervent seeking of the image of Jesus walking in that storm towards Peter, towards me, the light, the peace, shining around Him and the waters utterly calm wherever He is stepping.

THAT is the image I wrap my mind around when the splash and seduction of denial or ignorance or lack of humility and faith create the illusion of power that leads to death. I pray to keep my eyes on Jesus alone amidst the commotion, for in Him is the truth. In Him, I am free.

Lynn Quinn is a retired editor and religion teacher. She lives on Long Island and spends her retirement traveling around the world with her husband, Bill, and the Hibernian Singers.

THURSDAY OF THE FIFTH WEEK OF LENT
"In all truth I tell you, whoever keeps my word will never see death." John 8:51

YOU AND I KNOW ONE THING for certain: we will all die some day. There are different responses to the fact of death. Since we all die and everything dies and the universe will one day end, who cares how we live? Eat, drink and be merry for tomorrow we die. Or whoever dies with the most toys, wins. This is one way to face the reality of death. Look it in the eye and try to experience as much happiness as you possibly can in a lifetime. Many people live this way: for them, the goal of life is to be happy. Sounds reasonable.

Christianity offers a different response. You and I will die, but God's love is eternal and if we live in that love, we've found a way of life that doesn't die. It can't be killed. It lives on. Every day, we're invited to answer a different question: not will we die, but how will we live? In his lifetime, Jesus was convinced that there are realities that do not die, that cannot be killed. He invited people to live on that path or as John puts it in today's gospel, to "keep his word." In the church, those who have been faithful to Christ's word are part of the communion of saints. They are the dead who live on among us. By keeping alive their memory and spirit, the community of faith bring them back from the dead. Not only do they live on in God, but they live for us, as well.

Each saint in the communion is meant to be a manifestation of Christ for us in ways that Jesus himself may not have been able to do on his own. In every female saint, we gain a glimpse of the feminine incarnation of God's love in ways that Jesus would not have been able to reveal to us. In Mary, the Mother of God, we see the eternal yes to God's word. But saints are more than the official list of the canonized. They might include your Aunt Sophie or your grandfather. Saints, simply put are those whose faith, hope and love motivated their lives and whose examples will live on for us. It is the task of the church to keep alive the memory of its great saints for the whole community. They provide us with constant role models of discipleship. They remind us of what the church is called to be. It is the task of families to keep alive the memories of its domestic saints as well, honoring their examples set for us.

Jesus promises his followers that life can transcend death for those who are willing to be true to his word. The goal of every baptized Christian is to become his or her unique way of being a saint—not a plaster statue but a vibrant, living, loving, fully alive human being who listens to Christ and follows his word.

Greg Hagen is a martial arts instructor. He keeps a statue of St. Gregory the Great in his office.

FRIDAY OF THE FIFTH WEEK OF LENT

"I called to Yahweh in my anguish, I cried for help to my God; from his Temple he heard my voice, my cry came to his ears."
                                                                  Psalm 18:6

THE DEFINING MOMENT of my life came when I was eight years old and my father took his own life. Although more than four decades have passed since, and my life has been blessed in so many ways, it is still that moment that I recall when I hear the psalmist say "I called out to God in my anguish." I wrote this poem on the anniversary of my father's death some years ago, which always lands somewhere in Lent.

    Evolution or Abba?

    Out of the sea it all came.
    From those amniotic waters
        the soul came climbing high upon the heights
            And set her gaze wide
            and cried out "I" and "we" and "I love you"

    And on a dark, dark night, she has thrown herself
        from the cliffs
    and crashed upon the rocks
        And lies bloody and brainspilled.

The wretched body found, we cry out "NO"—
   A wordless NO, a cry without a voice.

Is there a grand scheme of things—
   and this day will play its part?
Will the sea bathe all in her salted tears
   and bring us home?

Tony Marinelli

SATURDAY OF THE FIFTH WEEK OF LENT
"I shall be their God, and they will be my people."
Ezekiel 37:27

SOMETIMES I FORGET that Christian faith grew out of Judaism. The Old Testament tells us that the Jews were the chosen people, called by God into a unique relationship with their Creator. Nothing like a little pressure.

At the heart of that covenant relationship, the idea that they were God's people, are two things: the Torah and the Sabbath. Together, they have kept the Jewish people , "a people" and kept them bonded to their God.

Our best friends are Orthodox Jews. In the hurried-ness of our lives, I've heard them say on a number of occasions, "I can't wait for shabbos." For them, sundown on Friday night brings home a welcomed rest, a time of prayer, a time for family and re-creation. Their Sabbath is what God's Sabbath was meant to be: a time to put aside things that are important, like school and work, for things that are even more important, things like prayer, study and recognition that God created this world, not the networks, not the banks, not the politicians.

Christians could desperately use an experience of Sabbath, a full 24 hours devoted to God, to studying scripture, to prayer and communal re-creation. We squeeze in a 40-minute Mass and then head for the golf course, the beach or the mall. Of course, the Eucharist is at the core of our prayer and worship but one Mass does not a Sabbath make.

Pope John Paul II recently wrote an apostolic letter on the importance of the Eucharist and Sunday worship. In it, he explained that Sunday is meant to be a special day for Christians. Each Sunday is a mini-Easter, a celebration of the Resurrection. He encouraged Catholics to use Sundays as a Christian Sabbath: to worship, spend time with family, celebrate your love for one another, visit the sick or the elderly who live alone.

At the heart of Sabbath is time: time for God, self, and community. Each day can contain within it a small sabbath experience. Individually, we might begin the day with Mass, or set aside some time for prayer or spiritual reading. I like to take a brisk walk every evening. I listen to a tape or meditative music while I walk. That's my Sabbath.

Lent is like a 40-day Sabbath, an extended time to re-orient my life, re-create my tired spiritual life as well as my relationships with family and members of my faith community, and re-order my priorities. God first.

Dave Bennigan lives on the upper west side of Manhattan, right next door to the Rosenberg family.

PASSION SUNDAY

EVERY YEAR AROUND THIS TIME, there are evenings of reflection given on the seven last words of Christ. The seven words actually refer to the seven statements made by Jesus on the cross. Different gospels tell slightly different versions of the crucifixion. Mark's gospel tells us that Jesus spoke only once on the cross. He prays the words in Psalm 22: *"Eli, Eli, lama sabacthani"* translated to mean "My God, my God, why have you abandoned me?"

Jesus has been betrayed by one of his disciples; others ran away. The Romans have beaten him and crowned him with thorns pushed into his skull. He has been tied and nailed to a cross where he hangs for three hours dying: "My God, my God why have you abandoned me?"

Jane is a forty-two-year-old woman who has three children ages 8 through 16. She wakes up one day to discover that her husband is leaving her. She has not worked in 16 years and has no real job skills. Now she has no husband: "My God my God why have you abandoned me?"

Alice is 84 years old and lies in a god-awful nursing home listening to the howls around her. No one visits. Not ever. Her daughter lives three thousand miles away in California and sends her cards and letters occasionally, but her daily experience is one of utter desolation: "My God my God why have you abandoned me?"

Robert is seventy and recently retired. He and his wife have been preparing for these days for years. They both love to travel and now is the time that they planned to do so. But his wife of forty six years is diagnosed with Alzheimers and is rapidly deteriorating. He cares for her with love each day but she has begun to forget who he is: "My God , my God why have you abandoned me?"

How could the last words of Jesus be words of abandonment? How could the Son of God cry out to God this way? How could he not? The mind boggling belief of Christian faith is that God entered into our humanity and has taken on all our sorrows.

My God my God why have you abandoned me? These may be the last words of Jesus, but they certainly aren't the last word from God. The Resurrection is the last word from God. In the midst of our darkest night is the absolute promise of a new dawn. Lord, this year, make me an instrument of your Resurrection, a sign of hope to the lonely, the poor, the sick and the dying. Into your hands, let me commit my spirit.

Tony Marinelli

MONDAY OF HOLY WEEK

"Meanwhile a large number of Jews heard that he was there and came not only on account of Jesus but also to see Lazarus whom he had raised from the dead."   *John 12:9-10*

PEOPLE LONGED TO BE NEAR LAZARUS. Maybe because he embodied the tension between life and death. Maybe they wanted to see what resurrection looked like. So do I.

We move through the forty days of Lent knowing what to expect on Easter. Pictures on holy cards and church walls portray the image of a resurrected Jesus wrapped in white garb with his arms extended, having defeated death. But the apostles didn't recognize the resurrected Christ. I wonder if we do? What does the Resurrection look like today in modern times?

Soldiers liberating Auchwitz? Does it look like hunger fed? The face of a starving child who has received his first meal in months? The Red Cross dropping medical supplies in a war torn country or in a nation that has experienced flooding or an earthquake? Two towers of light that shone in New York where the World Trade Center once stood? Millions of dollars donated to the families who lost a loved one on 9–11? The Body of Christ being distributed to the Body of Christ on Sunday?

What does resurrection look like? People gathered around Lazarus to see. We need not look far.

It's anywhere that despair finds hope, where the hungry are fed and the naked clothed. It's where addiction finds sobriety and sin finds mercy. It's wherever death finds new life.

Candy Gibbons traveled with the Jesuit Volunteer Corps to work with the poor. She entitled her journal of the experience, Spying Resurrection.

TUESDAY OF HOLY WEEK

"In all truth I tell you, one of you is going to betray me."   John 13:21

MY NEIGHBOR WAS RAISED in Holland. His family was Jewish and in danger of being arrested by Nazi soldiers. Christian neighbors hid his family for three months in the basement of their family's business. For a price, both families were betrayed by another neighbor. The families were arrested and sent to concentration camps. Miraculously, both families survived.

Many years later, both families found their way to America. So did their betrayer. He owned a profitable jewelry store in Brooklyn. One reason it was so profitable is that he sold imitation pearls and gems as the real thing. His ruse was eventually discovered, quite accidentally, by my neighbor, who he had betrayed during the war. The jeweler offered him a cut of the profits. He refused. The jeweler offered him cash. My neighbor refused again. The jeweler offered to make a large donation to the synagogue. Again, my neighbor refused his offer. The jeweler liquidated his business and gave the property, which he owned, to a Jewish organization, that to this day, rescues Jews from Russia.

My neighbor heard that the jeweler died penniless a few years later. *"And now Yahweh has spoke"* today's reading from Isaiah tells us. These words were later inscribed on the inner wall of what was once a place of betrayal and sin, now a place of hope and resurrection for Russian Jews.

George Povlitus lives in Queens, New York, right next door to the Bitterman family of Holland.

WEDNESDAY OF HOLY WEEK

"They paid him thirty pieces of silver, and from then onwards he kept looking for an opportunity to hand him over." Matthew 26:16

I once heard a story, fictional, of course, about a suicide note left behind by Judas. In the letter, he claims to have hurried along the process of our redemption by turning Jesus over to the authorities. The thirty pieces of silver were incidental, he reportedly wrote in the letter. Judas knew he would never live long enough to spend the money. He betrayed Jesus because someone had to, otherwise the story of salvation would never have been told.

Was the betrayal part of God's plan for our redemption? Had Judas not been deceptive, would the story of Jesus have ended differently?

We are, by nature, deceptive. That's how humankind has survived. From the beginning of time, the cavemen deceived the prey that fell to their sly hunting skills, the victors deceived the enemy in battle, cops have outwitted criminals and parents have placed the toys under the Christmas tree. Psychologists tell us that self-deception is used to defend our worst behaviors and addictions. I know. I'm an alcoholic. I abused alcohol for years. I also abused my wife and children. I was able to fool myself into thinking that everybody drinks; I'm not too drunk to drive; I can drink as much as I want and still be a good husband and father. But then, one cold March night, I was driving home drunk and fell asleep at the wheel. I walked away unharmed. The couple in the other car didn't.

The ability to deceive myself cost someone else dearly, and yet, through their forgiveness, and subsequently, my ability to forgive myself, I was redeemed. Would the story of salvation have played out differently had Judas not betrayed Jesus? Would my story of salvation been written differently had my sin not crossed paths with deeply compassionate people?

Every year, when the story of Judas' betrayal of Jesus is read from the altar, I think about the ways in which I betrayed myself, my marriage, my kids, and my God. Don't judge Judas too harshly. I suspect we all have at least one thing in common with him, the incredible ability to deceive and betray ourselves, others and the God who made us all.

Mick Mulrooney lives a sober, love-filled life committed to compassion. He is an active member of Alcoholics Anonymous, which for many, is an experience of resurrection.

HOLY THURSDAY   *John 13:1-15*

JOHN THE EVANGELIST TELLS US that Jesus knew the hour had come for him to pass from this world to the Father. On the way to Jerusalem and to his death, Jesus celebrates a rather special meal with his dear friends. John says that it provided an opportunity for Jesus to show how perfect his love was.

John writes his gospel after the other gospel accounts have circulated among the Christian communities of the time. He tends to write a more reflective account with fewer details and events than are contained in the other gospels. At the Last Supper, John offers rich reflections on the meaning and purpose of Christ's life. He doesn't recount the sharing of bread and wine and their eucharistic implications. The other gospel accounts have already provided this. He does offer a long discourse by Jesus and one event that is particular to his account. The washing of the feet summarizes in action and symbol all that Jesus has said and done in his life and ministry. It also expresses the significance of the Eucharist: the pouring out of love and service in the offering of his body and blood.

In the midst of their eating together, as they share their stories and perhaps forget for a moment the gathering storm that will threaten their company, Jesus gets up from the table, removes his outer garment, puts a towel around his waist and some water in a bucket. Notice, no words have been spoken. Can you see the look of confusion on the disciples' faces? He begins to wash their feet and wipe them with the towel he was wearing. Still, no words are spoken. It seems that some of the disciples simply let Jesus wash their feet.

Then he comes to Peter and it's no surprise that he's the one who objects.

"Lord, are you going to wash my feet?" Jesus answered. "At the moment you do not know what I am doing, but later you will understand."

"Never!" said Peter, "You shall never wash my feet." Jesus replied, "If I do not wash you, you can have no share with me."

Whose feet do you need to wash in order to become more like Christ? In order to grow as a person of integrity, or in order to develop the capacity of forgiveness, or in order to step beyond your hurt or wash away your anger or your bitterness, whose feet do you need to wash?

Are people as grateful as you would like them to be or as timely in their affirmation as you need them to be? Resentment can build up with family and friends and cause a wall of separation. Parents don't love each of their children in the same way. Teachers and mentors are not equal in their attention to their students. Are you envious or jealous of anyone in your life? Maybe this is the person whose feet you might wash.

Peter was impulsive and headstrong. He probably had strong feelings for or against people. If you are like Peter, there are probably people outside your vision whom you don't even notice or people you notice and dismiss. They might be poor or foreign-born, different from you in one way or another.

But they are also sitting at the table. Can you remain at the table without washing their feet?

"If I, the Lord and Master, have washed your feet, you must wash each other's feet. I have given you an example so that you may copy what I have done to you."

Monsignor Jim McNamara is the pastor of Holy Cross Parish in Nesconset, New York. He is a regular columnist for The Long Island Catholic *as well as the author of* In the Presence of the Wise and Gentle Christ *(Paulist Press, 1993).*

GOOD FRIDAY   *John 18:1–19:42*

I am only one, but still I am one. I cannot do everything, but still I can do something. I will not refuse to do the something I can do.—Helen Keller

JESUS AND MY SON, John, were both condemned to die. Jesus was executed, but John's life was spared. Jesus' mother, Mary, loved Jesus as much as I love my son—that unconditional kind of love that mothers have for children just because they were born. God loves each one of us that way, even though we haven't earned it and many times don't deserve it.

John, like Jesus, was also born to an unmarried mother. John is also a son of God, but his mother could not keep him. John was shuffled around in an inadequate foster care system the first year and a half of his life. When we adopted him, he finally had a family who would love and try to protect him forever.

John didn't learn in school or from his mistakes, he took things that didn't belong to him, and he told tall tales. As his mother, I did everything I could to guide John into responsible adulthood. As John grew older, his problems got larger and no matter where I turned, no one could help John and he didn't seem able to help himself. Eventually, he was sent to prison. Although John had never been violent, he escaped from prison and took two lives. When John was sentenced to death, my spirit went to death row.

After Jesus was sentenced to death, he was systematically dehumanized. The guards even gambled for his clothing. Mary suffered as she bore witness to the taunting and humiliation of her only son. Her heart must have broken. She could not protect Jesus or stop the machinery of death from grinding forward. As any mother, she would have done anything—given her own life—to save him.

Mary, as every mother of the condemned since her time, understood all too well that Jesus had been caught in a political web. He was innocent, but as a teacher he was misunderstood and feared by those who called out for his execution. The crowd was angry and thirsty for violence.

My son, John is not innocent. Although I continue to stand by him and love him, there is no way I could ever condone his violent crime. John's death sentence was also a political act. Being sent to death row depends on the status and the race of the victim, the quality of the defense lawyer, and other political variables.

The death penalty has never deterred crime. If it did, we would be a crime-free society by now. Capital punishment is predicated upon the principle of revenge which contributes to the cycle of violence, creates more victims, and is an unnecessary, barbaric practice.

I lost all hope and my faith was bruised when John was sentenced to death. Mary surely had moments where her own faith faltered. Could there be a God who lacked compassion? While John was still on death row, I came to understand that God does still love John unconditionally even though John has done the unspeakable.

John was fortunate. His soul has been allowed to grow. A compassionate re-sentencing judge changed his death sentence to life imprisonment when he learned that John's biological mother had a serious drinking problem. John was diagnosed as an adult with fetal alcohol syndrome (a brain disorder which occurred in the womb) and a string of genetic disorders over which he had no control.

Today, I believe God calls me to work for abolition of the death penalty. Mary would join the call to stop executions. She understood that when we do not speak, we cannot be heard.

The Lenten lesson for me is to practice love, compassion and mercy not just during the forty days before Easter —but as a daily practice.

Katherine Norgard is the mother of five children. She is a practicing psychologist in Arizona and works in a variety of ways to bring about abolition of the death penalty.

HOLY SATURDAY

IT IS HOLY SATURDAY MORNING, and my wife and I are walking down to the coffee shop we usually visit on weekends. There we will each pour ourselves a large cup of dark roast, and possibly a refill or two. As on nearly every other day this Lent, this will be our only "meal" until dinnertime. Watching me lace my coffee with plenty of cream, Mary gives me that bemused look that I often interpret—wrongly, she insists—as a sign of spiritual superiority. "I'm taking mine black during Lent," she wordlessly reminds me.

Mary and I had decided a week or so before Ash Wednesday that we would ratchet things up a bit this year. Last year we had given up meat for Lent, so this year, in addition to going meatless (and fishless, for that matter), we would confine ourselves to one meal at night. I decided to reserve the right to drink juices during the day, if my blood sugar levels seemed out of whack, and while Mary has accused me of pureeing a ham sandwich and a bag of sour cream potato chips in order to meet the letter of the law, I vigorously insist that it's only been carrots, apples, and celery. That's my story, and I'm sticking to it.

We sit and nurse our coffee and reflect on the last forty days. During previous Lents, neither of us had done much in the way of "giving up." As a schoolchild, I had followed the obligatory practice of giving up candy once or twice. But since I always associated that habit with those kids who seemed to flaunt their piety just a little too publicly, in the end I usually caved in long before Holy Week and gobbled down a Snickers bar in the privacy of my room. Aside from the mandated days of Lenten fast and abstinence, I had never tried anything this ambitious before, as my waistline amply testified.

Drinking our coffee and looking back at the past 40-some days, however, my wife and I both admit that in many ways we're going to miss the experience. The first few days were difficult. In the morning we often felt light-headed, but the hunger pangs were manageable until about mid-afternoon, when every third thought turned to food. A friend had told me that it was helpful to her, at times like that, to think about all those who wake up and go to bed hungry each day, and indeed those thoughts helped put our hunger in perspective, but we still found ourselves counting the hours till dinnertime.

As the days wore on, however, we grew more comfortable with the feelings of lightness and emptiness and instead of focusing on our deprivations, we began to celebrate in a more profound way the one meal we had. Dinnertime became a feast, albeit a meatless, fishless one. We shopped and cooked together, and set our table with a flourish. New pastas, soups, salads materialized. One night felafel, yogurt, tomatoes. Another night bountiful bean- and corn-filled tortillas. Always a plate of dates and cheese for dessert. We sat, we nibbled, we lingered in each other's company.

Instead of seeing our fast as a form of penitence, we realized that it was an opportunity to *pay attention* in a different sort of way. And in that way we drew support from the ancient Fathers of the Church who always spoke of fasting as an aid to prayer, not as an end in itself. By fasting we were not attempting to punish the flesh, we discovered, but to open our hearts to God by attending more carefully to the abundance of His gifts, for which we tried to give thanks each night in a more heartfelt way.

Fasting allowed us to pay attention to other things, as well: to how habits limit our imagination, and thus, our ability; to how spiritually hungry and impoverished we are; to the amazing physical bounty that we are blinded to because of the sheer surfeit of it. The list goes on.

Walking home from the café, we pass by our parish church. Tonight we will return here for the Easter vigil service, which reminds me of a friend who had called earlier in the week. Her husband, who has just finished the RCIA program, will be taking Holy Communion for the first time tonight at their parish several hundred miles away. "Do not work for food that cannot last," Jesus told us, "but for food that endures to eternal life" (John 6:27). Fasting for us was one step toward clearing away the clutter of all those distracting gods that keep us from recognizing, in small and large ways, those spiritual meals that God puts before us daily, but that we are too busy to see. And eat.

Thomas Grady has been an editor and publisher for many years and is now a literary agent who specializes in books on religion and spirituality. He is the co-editor of Signatures of Grace: Catholic Writers on the Sacraments *(Dutton, 2000). Mary Cichy Grady has been a teacher and a freelance writer. She now edits a newsletter on education issues for the state of California. The Gradys have two teenage children and live in northern California.*

EASTER

I REMEMBER A WINTER when the area where I lived was struck by an ice storm. Everything I looked at was coated with frozen glass. Tree branches encapsulated with ice arched to form sculptures that turned the whole area into one vast, magnificent art show. For a brief while I was seduced by this artificial beauty.

But very soon, the coldness emanating from it blasted me, and the chill was caused by more than temperature. It came from the knowledge that this apparent beauty really held betrayal. The ice had stopped the motion of the world. Everything was stilled. Movement and growth had been suspended. In reality, the illusion of beauty was the reality of death.

In the midst of this frozen world, I found myself longing for spring when the earth stirs in its very roots to begin its burst of new life in nature. But even more, I yearned for Easter, with its promise that death is not forever. For, in fact, the stillness of the ice had become, for me, Good Friday, that terrible day when we had put the Son of God to death and distanced ourselves from the Father. That act had left us orphaned, abandoned, encased in ice, until the Father gifted us again, giving us Easter, the miracle that life would return. The motionless ice would melt.

Years ago, when I was a child in a Catholic school, one of my nun-teachers made us write a composition on What Easter Means to Me. I remember writing that Easter promised that the sun would shine again and again even after days and days of rain. I think I'd write the same answer today, only now I'd say "even after days of ice," with ice defined as all the deaths I've risen from in these years.

That may sound dramatic, but whose life is without deaths, the Lents we must walk through, the Good Fridays where we each must struggle to come down from our cross, or be immobilized forever? All of us spend a lot of time in mourning, for life is full of ice storms—the son killed in an auto accident, the parent degenerating into senility, the depression which comes at passage times of our life, the loss of a job, the break-up of a relationship, the drying up of faith, the death of ideals, innocence, hopes and dreams. I have done my intense Good Friday mourning for a son, driven to suicide by a flawed brain, and for a son and daughter-in-law murdered by an amoral youth. I have known the sterile, frozen Lent that broken hearts are destined to enter, and the Good Friday where we die on a Cross with our Lord.

But Easter comes, with its promise of rebirth, not just from the ultimate act of physical death, but rebirth from the many Lents and Good Fridays we have to deal with in life. Easter taught me that all these deaths remain an enemy only when—like an ice storm—we let them trap us into immobility instead of believing its promise of new-life, assuring us that every death is a fraud. For inherent in every death is the wonderful crisis of birth. The hard part is to believe that when we're lost in Lent.

Understanding Lent doesn't come easy. It doesn't make sense until we really see what it is leading to—Easter, the event in which all the mysteries of life are contained, the drama of life and death itself, ending not with frozen immobility, but with the regeneration of life. Jesus' mission and message was to show people for all time that

Life triumphs, that death can be thawed and new life spring from it, not by wishing, but by loving. To get that message across, there had to be a Lent and Good Friday, before there could be an Easter.

It's not easy to write about Lent and Easter. This sequence shakes both the earth and the heavens for Christians, because it contains all the dramas of existence and mysteries of Creation. It is about the explosion of God out to humankind and the synthesis of humankind with God. This can't be expressed in ordinary language or popular style. How can we communicate an understanding of a truth which can only be grasped from the depths of one's soul?

Yet, humbly, I have felt the melting ice which has enabled me to accept the pain/joy, failure/conquering, death/rebirth contrasts of Lent and Easter. And I marvel with gratitude as I have come to learn that Lent and Easter are all about the mystery of a Divine promise—Love conquers all deaths.

Antoinette Bosco, a syndicated columnist for Catholic News Service, *is the author of nine books, the latest being* "Choosing Mercy, A Mother of Murder Victims Pleads to End the Death Penalty" *(Orbis Books).*

❋ *Especially for Lent & Easter* ❋

Mitch Finley
SEASON OF NEW BEGINNINGS
Praying Through Lent with Dorothy Day, St. Teresa of Avila, St. Augustine, and Other Spiritual Masters

A literary sparkplug, to keep the spirit of Lent alive for you one day at a time.

RP590/04   1-878718-32-0 $4.95

Francis X. Gaeta
WHAT HE DID FOR LOVE
Our Companion for the Forty Days of Lent
Foreword by Thelma Hall, r.c.

". . . teaches a genuine Christ-centered spirituality."
— THELMA HALL, R.C.

RP101/04   1-878718-41-X $5.95

Francis X. Gaeta
THE GREAT FIFTY DAYS
Savoring the Resurrection
Foreword by Joseph F. Girzone

". . . continually nourishes as it offers deeper insights into the life of Jesus and our relationship with him."
— From the Foreword by JOSEPH F. GIRZONE, author of *Joshua*

RP125/04   1-878718-58-4 $5.95

Judy Marley
BEHOLD THE MAN
Meditations on the Passion, Death and Resurrection of Jesus

An invitation to an unforgettable journey with Jesus.
RP030/04   0-9623410-2-9 $4.50

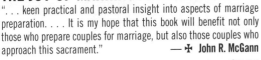

Also by the Author

Tony Marinelli and Pat McDonough
THE JOY OF MARRIAGE PREPARATION
". . . keen practical and pastoral insight into aspects of marriage preparation. . . . It is my hope that this book will benefit not only those who prepare couples for marriage, but also those couples who approach this sacrament."   — ✠ John R. McGann

No. RP 148/04   1-878718-64-9 $5.95

Additional Titles Published by Resurrection Press, a Catholic Book Publishing Imprint

A Rachel Rosary *Larry Kupferman*	$4.50
Blessings All Around *Dolores Leckey*	$8.95
Catholic Is Wonderful *Mitch Finley*	$4.95
Come, Celebrate Jesus! *Francis X. Gaeta*	$4.95
Days of Intense Emotion *Keeler/Moses*	$12.95
From Holy Hour to Happy Hour *Francis X. Gaeta*	$7.95
Grace Notes *Lorraine Murray*	$9.95
Healing through the Mass *Robert DeGrandis, SSJ*	$9.95
Our Grounds for Hope *Fulton J. Sheen*	$7.95
The Healing Rosary *Mike D.*	$5.95
Healing Your Grief *Ruthann Williams, OP*	$7.95
Life, Love and Laughter *Jim Vlaun*	$7.95
Living Each Day by the Power of Faith *Barbara Ryan*	$8.95
Loving Yourself for God's Sake *Adolfo Quezada*	$5.95
The Joy of Being an Altar Server *Joseph Champlin*	$5.95
The Joy of Being a Catechist *Gloria Durka*	$4.95
The Joy of Being a Eucharistic Minister *Mitch Finley*	$5.95
The Joy of Being a Lector *Mitch Finley*	$5.95
The Joy of Being an Usher *Gretchen Hailer, RSHM*	$5.95
The Joy of Marriage Preparation *McDonough/Marinelli*	$5.95
The Joy of Music Ministry *J.M. Talbot*	$6.95
The Joy of Preaching *Rod Damico*	$6.95
The Joy of Teaching *Joanmarie Smith*	$5.95
The Joy of Worshiping Together *Rod Damico*	$5.95
Lights in the Darkness *Ave Clark, O.P.*	$8.95
Meditations for Survivors of Suicide *Joni Woelfel*	$8.95
Mother Teresa *Eugene Palumbo, S.D.B.*	$5.95
Personally Speaking *Jim Lisante*	$8.95
Practicing the Prayer of Presence *Muto/van Kaam*	$8.95
Prayers from a Seasoned Heart *Joanne Decker*	$8.95
Praying the Lord's Prayer with Mary *Muto/van Kaam*	$8.95
Praying through Our Lifetraps *John Cecero, SJ*	$9.95
Rising from the Ashes *Adolfo Quezada*	$4.95
5-Minute Miracles *Linda Schubert*	$4.95
Season of New Beginnings *Mitch Finley*	$4.95
Season of Promises *Mitch Finley*	$4.95
St. Katharine Drexel *Daniel McSheffery*	$12.95
Stay with Us *John Mullin, SJ*	$3.95
Surprising Mary *Mitch Finley*	$7.95
What He Did for Love *Francis X. Gaeta*	$5.95
Woman Soul *Pat Duffy, OP*	$7.95
You Are My Beloved *Mitch Finley*	$10.95

For a free catalog call 1-800-892-6657
Visit our website: www.catholicbookpublishing.com